Other titles in the series

Basic
Learning
Processes
in
Childhood

Basic
Learning
Processes
in
Childhood

Hayne W. Reese

West Virginia University

Holt, Rinehart and Winston

New York, Chicago, San Francisco, Atlanta, Dallas,
Montreal, Toronto, London, Sydney

Foreword

The Principles of Educational Psychology Series

The materials used to present educational psychology to teachers should have two dominant characteristics—excellence and adaptability. The *Principles of Educational Psychology Series* aspires to both. It consists of several short books, each devoted to an essential topic in the field. The authors of the books are responsible for their excellence; each author is noted for a command of his or her topic and for a deep conviction of the importance of the topic for teachers. Taken as a whole, the series provides comprehensive coverage of the major topics in educational psychology, but it is by no means a survey, for every topic is illuminated in a distinctive way by the individual approach of each author.

Numerous considerations require that the materials used

for instruction in educational psychology be adaptable. One consideration is that the readership is heterogeneous, including students in pre-service teacher training programs, of whom some have and others have not taken prior work in psychology, as well as professional teachers in in-service programs who have already completed previous courses in educational psychology. The separate booklets in the *Principles of Educational Psychology Series* are intended to be responsive to these differences. The writing is clear and direct, providing easy access for the novice, and the authors' fresh and distinctive viewpoints offer new insights to the more experienced.

Another consideration is that the format of courses in educational psychology varies widely. A course may be designed for pre-service or for in-service programs, for early childhood, elementary, secondary, or comprehensive programs, or to offer special preparation for teaching in urban, suburban, or rural settings. The course may occupy a full academic year, a semester, trimester, quarter, or an even shorter period. A common set of topics may be offered to all students in the course, or the topical coverage may be individualized. The *Principles of Educational Psychology Series* can be adapted to any one of these formats. Since the series consists of separate books, each one treating a single topic, instructors and students can choose to adopt the entire set or selected volumes from it, depending on the length, topical emphasis, and structure of the course.

The need for effective means of training teachers is of increasing urgency. To assist in meeting that need, the intent of the series is to provide materials for presenting educational psychology that are distinctive in approach, excellent in execution, and adaptable in use.

William Rohwer
Carol Rohwer
Series Editors
Berkeley, California
February, 1974

Preface

This book is an introduction to the psychological study of basic learning processes in children. We take an empirical approach, stressing the findings of laboratory research more than the theoretical interpretation of these findings. In another volume in this series, Gagné presents a theoretical analysis of learning and uses it to derive recommendations about classroom teaching. Here, we derive practical recommendations from the research findings. Our approach and Gagné's are complementary, and both can be useful to the prospective teacher.

This book was written for students who are not majors in psychology and who therefore do not have much familiarity with the technical vocabulary of psychology. Some technical terms are introduced, but their use is deliberate and based on the conviction that precise communication sometimes requires technical terms. In addition, any student who studies basic learning processes should acquire the basic technical vocabulary used by psychologists to discuss these processes.

Basic learning processes are the kinds of learning processes studied in the psychological laboratory, as opposed to the classroom or other natural setting. The purpose of studying these processes is to increase our understanding of how and why learning occurs and how the course of learning can be modified. The focus is on the learning *processes* themselves, rather than on the learning of any particular content matter. The processes are studied in the artificial laboratory setting rather than in the "real world," because in the laboratory it is possible to control many of the extraneous conditions that can influence performance in a learning task and can obscure the underlying processes. In general, then, the psychological study of basic learning processes is aimed at examining those processes in constrained, artificial, and relatively content-free situations. Nevertheless, much that is known about the basic learning processes seems to have important practical implications.

We have made no attempt in this book to review all of the studies of basic learning processes in large part because there are far too many studies to be covered in a book this size. In addition most of the details of such studies would be of interest only to experts in the area. Instead our intention was to show what is studied, how it is studied, what general facts have been discovered, and what these facts mean to the practitioner. Toward this end, we begin each chapter with a statement of the problem under consideration and end with suggestions about practical applications. In between, a sample study is described, and salient findings are surveyed. Finally, at the end of each chapter we have included a list of more technical writings that are recommended for further reading.

I wish to acknowledge my gratitude to Dr. Ralph R. Turner, for reacting to an earlier draft, and to my home institution, West Virginia University, for covering the many small expenses involved in the preparation of a manuscript, and most importantly for providing a secretary, Mrs. Margaret Swanson, whose work eased the task considerably. I am especially grateful to the editors of this series, William D. Rohwer, Jr., and Carol P. Rohwer, for their excellent detailed comments on a draft version of the book.

Hayne W. Reese
Morgantown, West Virginia
January 1976

Contents

Basic Learning Processes in Childhood

Chapter 1 Introduction

The study of learning processes is pervasive throughout psychology. There are well over 1500 published studies of learning in children, in addition to thousands of other published studies of learning in adults and the elderly. The reason so much effort has been expended in this area is that psychological processes are largely dependent on learning for their development and maintenance. Thus, in order to understand human behavior and development, we must first understand learning. The study of learning is important not only for psychologists but for educators as well because education is the application of the principles of learning.

Themes of the Book

The purpose of this book is to acquaint you with the methods and theories psychologists use in the study of learning, especially those relevant to classroom teaching. To achieve this end, we have organized each chapter as follows: first we define the problem covered, then we describe a representative study, summarizing its methods and findings, and finally we survey the salient findings of other research to provide an overview of the topic. Age differences are described when they are striking.

The book has two themes. The first is that even the most basic kinds of learning are influenced by cognitive processes or mental activities. In more complex kinds of learning the influence of cognition is even more apparent. The influence of cognitive processes is seen whenever your performance is affected by thinking or by making a decision. If you reflect about the solution to a problem or choose among alternatives, you are exercising your cognitive processes.

The other recurrent theme is that basic learning is related to the organization of the material to be learned. Interrelations among materials are important determinants of the ease of learning. For this reason, when faced with material that seems meaningless and unrelated, we often try to impose meaning and relatedness to make learning easier. Imposing meaning or relatedness is a cognitive process. Therefore the two themes are connected to each other through one underlying theme: the learner, even in basic learning situations, uses cognitive processes to seek meaning and orderliness in the world that confronts him.

How the Book is Organized

This book begins with the simplest kinds of learning and proceeds to the more complex. In Chapter 2 we will look at conditioning, which some people consider the simplest kind of learning. However, as you will see, conditioning may be simple only with respect to the experimental methods used. Chapter 3 deals with discriminative or discrimination learning. This term refers not to the learning of prejudice but rather to learning to select one object instead of another.

Actually, the learning of prejudice is relevant to the transfer of discriminative learning, which is examined in Chapter 4. As you will see in that chapter, discriminative transfer can be a relatively simple or complex process. One kind of discriminative transfer is considered the experimental analogue of responding on the basis of prejudice.

Chapter 5 deals with verbal learning and memory in a variety of tasks. One of these is paired-associate learning, which is essentially the same as learning a foreign-language vocabulary by pairing an English word with its foreign-language equivalent. Included in this chapter are discussions of several effective memory aids. In Chapter 6 we will examine the transfer of verbal learning. An important source of this transfer is mediation. That is, words or visual images which you use as memory aids in one task may be transferred to a second task where they may interfere with or facilitate second-task learning. Chapter 7 deals with other kinds of verbal learning and transfer, called conceptual processes, in which concepts are applied to solve problems.

In each of these chapters we have provided an overview of the experimental research and theoretical discussions related to each topic rather than an exhaustive study. In addition, although the topics covered represent only a sampling of the topics related to basic learning processes, they do cover those issues which we feel are most central. Many of the topics which we have not included are esoteric and of interest primarily to specialists.

We have touched only briefly in this book on one kind of learning that has immediate classroom application. This kind of learning, on which behavior modification is based, is covered more thoroughly in another book in this series (*Student Motivation and Behavior Modification* by Donald M. Baer). In addition, because specific school applications are dealt with in other volumes, they will not be considered here. Instead, we will look at the major categories of basic learning processes, emphasizing findings of both theoretical importance and practical application.

How References Are Organized

Most of the assertions made about research findings in this book are not documented by citation of references because we felt the citations would not be useful to the student who is more interested in the facts than in their sources. In addition, most of the assertions refer to well-documented findings which are apt to be known already to the student who is more expert in the area. However, some references are cited, and the style of these citations is that used in publications of the American Psychological Association. The author's name and the publication year of his work are given within the text. The full bibliographic listing for each cited work is provided after Chapter 7.

Each chapter ends with a list of suggested readings. These readings can provide you with further information, including documentation, about the topics covered. If you need still more information you could begin with these suggested readings and then use their bibliographies to track down other relevant material.

Terminology and Jargon

It is almost impossible for a psychologist to discuss his subject matter without using technical jargon. Though we have tried to keep this practice to a minimum here, some jargon could be avoided only by complicated circumlocutions.

Two terms that are basic to psychology and which are used extensively are stimulus and response. A *stimulus* is any object or event that excites sensory receptors. It can have its origin outside or inside the organism, because there are sensory receptors that are excitable by objects or events outside or inside the organism. Psychologists make a distinction between potential stimuli and effective stimuli. A *potential stimulus* is one that is capable of exciting sensory receptors but that has not yet done so. For example, is sound produced by a falling tree if no one is there to hear it? If "sound" means the effect of vibrations on auditory receptors, then the falling tree produces vibrations—potential stimuli—but these produce no "sound"—an *effective stimulus*—unless someone's auditory receptors are affected. Stimulation and cue are sometimes used as synonyms for stimulus.

The other term is response. A *response* is any activity of an organism, either physiological, neural, or motor. That is, a response can be the functioning of glands or nerves or it can be produced by muscle contractions. Synonyms for response include act, activity, function, reaction, and behavior.

In order for you to understand the psychologist's use of the word response, there are two other points of which you should be aware. First, the word *response* is derived from a Latin word meaning to promise in return or, more simply, to answer. Thus response implies, by its derivation, an answer to a stimulus. Reaction has a similar implication. However, psychologists use these terms in some situations where this implication is not intended. That is, they may speak of responses and reactions even when there appears to be no eliciting stimulus or stimulus to be answered. The second point that you should be aware of is that behavior is a synonym for response. Thus behavior does not have the same meaning in psychology that it has in everyday English, as in the admonishment, "Be on your good behavior."

Another useful term is *subject*. To psychologists, a subject is an organism whose behavior is being observed. In a study of classroom learning of fifth-grade children, the subjects of the study are the children, not the materials to be learned. This word may be confusing unless you keep in mind that the psychologist's primary interest is in the organism or its behavior, which is the true subject of study.

A Note on Practical Implications

Most of the "practical implications" that we will discuss in the following chapters have no supporting basis in research. There is, in fact, little research demonstrating that the principles will have the suggested effects in real-life settings. The reason is that most researchers who study basic learning processes have not been concerned with the possible practical implications or applications of their findings. Conversely, most researchers interested in learning in the classroom and other natural settings have not been concerned with the kinds of basic learning processes covered in this book.

One notable exception is the group of researchers who study operant learning and behavior modification. They have studied operant learning and behavior modification as basic learning processes and as educational and therapeutic techniques. However, their work is not covered extensively in this book, because, as already noted, it is covered in another volume in the series.

Except in the area of operant learning and behavior modification, then, there have been few studies of the practical application of basic learning principles. Therefore, you should consider the practical implications discussed here as hints or suggestions to be tried out, rather than as guidelines or principles that will necessarily work. The suggestions seem reasonable, however, and should be tried in classrooms and other natural settings in which they seem relevant. If a procedure does not work, perhaps it will work in another setting or in the same setting with modifications. Or perhaps another one will work. The test is in the attempted application.

Suggested Readings

Introduction to Basic Learning Processes

Bugelski, B. R. *The Psychology of Learning*. New York: Holt, Rinehart and Winston, 1956.

Methods of Studying Learning

Hilgard, E. R. Methods and procedures in the study of learning. In S. S. Stevens (Ed.), *Handbook of Experimental Psychology*. New York: Wiley, 1951. Pp. 517-612.

Chapter 2 Conditioning

The term *conditioning* refers to two simple kinds of procedures for the study of learning. One is *classical conditioning* and the other is *instrumental conditioning*. Classical conditioning is called *classical* because historically it is the first procedure that was developed. Instrumental conditioning is called *instrumental* because it is designed for the study of functional behavior or behavior that is instrumental in achieving some goal. Though the two procedures are simple, they are somewhat difficult to explain.

The Conditioning Procedures

Classical conditioning. In classical conditioning, a stimulus is presented, followed by a second stimulus that has been selected to elicit the response of interest. The second stimulus can be an "appetitive" stimulus, like food or water, or it can be an aversive stimulus, like an electric shock or a sudden loud sound. This second stimulus produces the response of interest. For example, food placed in the mouth produces salivation, or a sudden loud sound produces startle. The first stimulus can be any cue that prior to training had no tendency to arouse the response of interest. As a result of the temporal sequence of initial stimulus, followed by eliciting stimulus, followed by elicited response; the initial stimulus acquires the capacity to elicit the response.

The initial stimulus is a *signaling stimulus* because it signals the occurrence of the eliciting stimulus. It is also identified as a *conditioned* or *conditional stimulus*. The eliciting stimulus is identified as an *unconditioned stimulus*. The response elicited by the unconditioned stimulus is identified as an *unconditioned response*; and the response elicited by the conditioned stimulus after training is identified as the *conditioned response*. You can see that without any training the unconditioned stimulus elicits the unconditioned response. In contrast, without training the conditioned stimulus does not elicit the conditioned response. However, after training, the conditioned stimulus does elicit the conditioned response.

The following example may make this conditioning process clearer. Suppose the response to be conditioned is salivation. Because a tone has no tendency to elicit salivation, we can use it as the conditioned stimulus. Food placed in the mouth does elicit salivation, and therefore it can be used as the unconditioned stimulus. If we presented the tone (conditioned stimulus), then the food (unconditioned stimulus), the food would cause salivation (unconditioned response). However, after several repetitions of the sequence of tone and food, the tone alone would elicit salivation (conditioned response).

The unconditioned stimulus can be appetitive or aversive, as already noted. When it is appetitive, the procedure is called classical appetitive conditioning. The conditioning of salivation is an example, because the unconditioned stimulus (food) is an appetitive stimulus. When the unconditioned stimulus is aversive, the procedure is called classical aversive conditioning. An example of the latter would be conditioning the startle response. A sudden loud sound is an unconditioned stimulus for the startle response, and sudden loud sounds are aversive.

An important part of the classical conditioning procedure—whether appetitive or aversive—is that the unconditioned stimulus is presented at its appointed time whether or not the organism emits the conditioned response.

Instrumental conditioning. In instrumental conditioning no eliciting stimulus (unconditioned stimulus) is presented, and there may or may not be a signaling stimulus (conditioned stimulus). The essential feature of the instrumental conditioning procedure is that the presentation of a stimulus depends on what the organism does. Thus the stimulus is contingent upon the occurrence of the response. Because the contingent stimulus can be appetitive or aversive, there is instrumental appetitive and instrumental aversive conditioning. In instrumental appetitive conditioning the occurrence of the response is followed by a reward. For example, pulling a lever (response) could be followed by the delivery of candy (reward).

There are two types of instrumental aversive conditioning. In one, called instrumental avoidance conditioning, a signal is presented to warn the subject that the aversive stimulus is about to be presented. If the subject responds in time, the aversive stimulus is not presented. Thus, by responding the subject *avoids* the aversive stimulus. For example, a tone might signal that electric shock will be presented unless a lever is pulled immediately.

In the other type, instrumental escape conditioning, there is no warning signal. The aversive stimulus is presented unexpectedly, but the occurrence of the response terminates the stimulus. Thus, the subject *escapes* from the aversive stimulus by responding. For example, electric shock might be presented without warning but terminated when a lever is pulled.

In the examples for both types of instrumental aversive

conditioning, the consequence of not responding was aversive stimulation. The withdrawal of positive stimuli can also serve as an aversive consequence. For example, pleasant music might be terminated unless the response occurs. This instrumental aversive procedure is sometimes called response-cost or omission training.

In all of the instrumental conditioning procedures, the contingent stimulus can be dependent on the *non*occurrence of the response instead of on the occurrence of the response. In response-cost training, for instance, the music might be terminated whenever the response does not occur.

Extinction.   The opposite of conditioning is *extinction*. Extinction means that by the application of a particular experimental procedure, the strength of a conditioned response is reduced until eventually it disappears completely. The experimental procedure consists of presenting the conditioned stimulus without the unconditioned stimulus in classical conditioning and omitting the contingent stimulus following the response in instrumental conditioning.

Kinds of responses.   The response in classical conditioning is sometimes called a *respondent* and the response in instrumental conditioning, an *operant*. A respondent is an *elicited* response and an operant is an *emitted* response. Elicited responses occur only if the appropriate eliciting stimulus occurs. Emitted responses occur in the absence of any eliciting stimulus. The eyeblink produced by a sudden flash of bright light is elicited and therefore is a respondent. Talking is not elicited and is therefore an operant response. Later we will see that the occurrence of an operant response, such as talking, can be encouraged by the presence of appropriate stimuli, such as other persons, but these stimuli do not *elicit* the response.

Classical Conditioning

Almost all of the research on classical conditioning in human subjects has been done with young infants or college students. An example of a well-designed study using infants is an experiment by Lipsitt, Kaye, and Bosack (1966). The subjects of this study were newborn infants, 1-½ to 4 days old, and the purpose was to see whether classical conditioning is possible at this age. The response selected for study was sucking. The conditioned stimulus was placing the end of a flexible rubber tube into the infant's mouth. The unconditioned stimulus was sweetened water delivered through the tube (about a teaspoonful each time), which produced the unconditioned response, sucking. That is, when the sweetened water entered the infant's mouth, he automatically began to make sucking movements. In the conditioning procedure, the tube (conditioned stimulus) was placed in the infant's mouth for 15 seconds, and during the last 5 seconds of this period the sweetened water was delivered. Various control conditions were included, and it was found that the conditioning procedure increased the amount of sucking on the tube. In a final session the sweetened water was no longer presented through the tube, and the amount of tube sucking declined.

This study demonstrates classical conditioning in newborn infants, and it is therefore of technical interest. It appears to excite little practical interest, however, because a similar kind of classical conditioning occurs in nature without any prior planning. Infants who are bottle-fed usually learn very quickly to stop crying when they see the bottle being brought to them or even when they hear the noises that accompany the bottle's preparation. The cessation of crying is viewed as a classically conditioned response. Before any training, the sight of the bottle is neutral, and the infant will continue to cry until the nipple of the bottle is put into his mouth. However, the nipple in the mouth is the unconditoned stimulus for sucking, and sucking is incompatible with crying. The infant cannot suck and cry at the same time, and therefore, because sucking is unconditionally produced by the nipple in the mouth, the cessation of crying is also unconditionally produced by the nipple in the mouth. Thus, there are two unconditioned responses (sucking and not crying) to the one unconditioned stimulus. These responses are conditionable.

That is, they can become conditioned to the previously neutral stimulus, the sight of the bottle. Consequently, the sight of the bottle can become, through classical conditioning, a conditioned stimulus for the cessation of crying and for incipient sucking movements.

You can see that classical conditioning to the sight of the bottle will occur naturally in bottle-fed babies unless the mother takes great care to prevent it. She could, of course, try to make no noise in preparing the bottle, and she could quietly sneak up on the baby and suddenly stick the nipple into his mouth. By taking such precautions she could try to avoid presenting stimuli associated with the bottle and thus prevent conditioning. However, she would have no reason to prevent the conditioning unless she were a psychologist interested in this experiment. If the mother behaves normally when the baby is bottle-fed, the conditioned cessation of crying should develop with no extra effort or deliberate planning.

Cognition and conditioning. You may think that learning in the classical conditioning procedure is futile. The organism can neither prevent nor avoid the aversive stimulation, nor hasten the appetitive stimulation. These stimuli will be presented at their scheduled times regardless of whether the organism responds to the signaling stimulus. Nevertheless, learning does occur. In addition, it can be useful.

One area in which classical conditioning can be useful is cognition or mental activity. Cognition can influence classical conditioning, but classical conditioning can also influence cognition. The latter fact is what makes classical conditioning useful.

Some researchers have suggested that classical conditioning is more a matter of cognition than of pure learning (e.g., Sameroff, 1971, 1972). They argue that the conditioned response depends on the subject's being *aware* of the relationship between the conditioned stimulus and the unconditioned stimulus and on his choosing to respond in accordance with that relationship. It is known that awareness can influence the performance of adults in classical-conditioning situations (e.g., Spence, 1963). Thus, even though classical conditioning can be demonstrated in unaware subjects in whom it must therefore reflect pure learning and not cognition, the fact remains that cognition can influence classical conditioning.

It is also possible that cognition can be influenced by classical conditioning. This influence can be seen in techniques of psychotherapy based on the classical conditioning of cognitions (e.g., see Jacobs & Wolpin, 1971). For example, in one technique for treating phobias, or unreasonable fears, the patient is first trained to relax deeply. Then he is asked to imagine scenes that frighten him and at the same time is commanded to relax. Fear and relaxation cannot occur simultaneously; the patient cannot be afraid if he is relaxed. When the procedure is used correctly, the relaxed state becomes conditioned to the previously feared situations and prevents the occurrence of the fear response, thereby eliminating the phobia.

Another influence of classical conditioning in the cognitive realm is related to imagination. Many theorists conceive of the mental image as a classically conditioned sensation. According to these theorists, classical conditioning is the source of imagery. A sensation of an object is aroused by seeing the object. As a conditioned response, the *image* of an object is aroused by a stimulus—a conditioned stimulus—other than the object. For example, the aroma of burning hickory might produce images of camping trips you went on as a child because hickory was burned during those outings.

Classical conditioning, then, can have practical usefulness as a means for promoting mental health and as the source of mental imagery. Probably its most pervasive practical influence, however, is on emotional responses, which are believed to be classically conditionable.

Conditioning of emotions. In classical aversive conditioning, the unconditioned response is probably a complex set of behaviors. These include emotional components such as fear, as well as avoidance behaviors. Not only the avoidance behaviors, but also the emotional components, are conditioned to the signaling stimulus. Thus, as a result of conditioning, the organism learns not only to make tentative avoidance responses to the signaling stimulus, but also to fear it. Suppose as a child you were never sent to the principal's office except to be punished. Then classical conditioning should have occurred, because the signaling stimulus—the office—was followed by an aversive stimulus—the punishment—and you learned to fear the office, or being sent to the office. You learned to expect punishment in the office, and that expectation was associated with a fearful reaction. Such a learned fear response can spread to similar stimuli or situations, and you might have come to fear school, or being sent to school. It is doubtful, however, that such a pervasive fear would be learned unless the punishment experiences were frequent, severe, and not offset by pleasureable experiences.

Just as fear can be learned in classical aversive conditioning, positive emotional responses are believed to be conditionable in the classical appetitive situation. Stimulation associated with appetitive stimuli arouse, as the result of conditioning, an expectation that the appetitive stimuli, or rewards, will soon follow. This expectation is theoretically related to pleasurable emotions. It appears, therefore, that classical conditioning produces expectancies of reward or punishment, which are associated with positive or negative feelings.

This principle can be put to practical use. It is known that strong negative emotions can interfere with other learning. Therefore, it is desirable to avoid the conditioning of negative emotions to the classroom, where learning is supposed to occur. Consequently, when punishment is deemed to be necessary, it is desirable to have it administered in a situation different from the classroom. Insofar as possible, rewards should characterize the classroom, and punishment should be given elsewhere. Furthermore, in order to avoid the generalization of the learned fear response from the punishment situation to the classroom situation, these two should be made as distinctly different as possible. The one fly in the ointment is that it is also known that delay of reward or punishment retards learning. Thus, when punishment is not given in the classroom, where the undesirable behavior occurred, the behavior that is to be punished will be followed by a relatively long delay of punishment. As a result, the punishment will have little effect on the behavior that led to the punishment, and the only learning that is likely to occur is the conditioning of fear to the punishment situation.

Use of threats.   The conditioning of fear to a punishment situation can be useful. If being sent to the office arouses fear, then the threat of being sent to the office will also arouse fear. Since fear, like any negative emotion, is itself a kind of punishment, the threat of being sent to the office can be used as an immediate punishment for undesirable behavior. However, because of classical conditioning, a threatening teacher comes to be a feared teacher.

The conditioning of fear to the teacher exemplifies a procedure called *higher-order conditioning.* In such a procedure the eliciting stimulus is not a primary unconditioned stimulus, but rather it is a stimulus that because of previous conditioning has become a signaling stimulus. That is, as a result of conditioning, a neutral stimulus acquires the ability to elicit a particular response (in this case, fear). Subsequently, other stimuli systematically associated with that stimulus will, as a result of higher-order conditioning, also acquire the ability to elicit this response. In higher-order conditioning, in other words, a conditioned stimulus that has already acquired the capacity to arouse the response of interest is used instead of an unconditioned stimulus. The procedure is otherwise the same as standard classical conditioning.

In classical conditioning the learned response is not the same as the unconditioned response. The learned response is a *part* of the unconditioned response, but it is only that part which can occur in the absence of the eliciting stimulus. In the case of aversive conditioning, part of the unconditioned response to the aversive stimulus is fear, as already noted. This part can be conditioned. Another part of the unconditioned response is pain. But pain is caused by stimulation of pain receptors, and it cannot occur unless these receptors are stimulated. Therefore, the pain component of the unconditioned response cannot be conditioned. Consequently, the conditioned response must be in a sense weaker than the unconditioned response; the conditioned response includes fear but not pain.

If in higher-order aversive conditioning the new conditioned response is only a fraction of the original conditioned response, then the fear response learned through higher-order conditioning will be weaker than the fear response learned through presentation of an aversive stimulus. Thus, the threatening teacher would be feared, because of higher-order conditioning, but would not be feared as much as a punishing teacher.

To summarize: First, punishment leads to the conditioning of fear to the situation in which punishment is given. Second, fear can disrupt other learning. Therefore, since learning is supposed to occur in the classroom, it is undesirable to give punishment in the classroom. However, it is sometimes desireable to punish certain behaviors, yet if the punishment is not given immediately, it is not likely to affect the undesirable behavior. But even though delayed punishment does not affect the undesirable behavior, it does lead to the conditioning of fear to the punishment situation, and consequently it leads to the conditioning of fear to any signal that the punishment situation is impending. The threat to send a child to the punishment situation is such a signal, and therefore arouses fear. Because fear has aversive properties, the threat to send the child to the punishment situation is punishing and can be used in the classroom as a milder form of punishment. We have also seen that the threatening teacher will be feared, but not as much as a punishing teacher. Therefore, the fear produced by a threatening teacher should not be as disruptive of new learning as the fear produced by a punishing teacher.

We know, of course, that in order for this procedure to be successful, the threat must be followed by the deed whenever the threat alone fails to inhibit the undesired response. The teacher who threatens to send the child to the principal for punishment should always do so when the misbehavior occurs in spite of the threat. Classical conditioning occurs only on the occasions when the signaling stimulus is actually followed by the eliciting stimulus. When the eliciting stimulus is omitted, the tendency of the signaling stimulus to arouse the response is weakened. Omitting the eliciting stimulus is the extinction procedure. Thus, empty threats —threats not carried out in action—amount to an extinction procedure. In the present case, empty threats would result in a loss of credibility, a reduced fearfulness, and eventually a loss of the threat's effectiveness.

Use of promises.   In the preceding discussion it was suggested that the principles of classical aversive conditioning can be used to good advantage by a classroom teacher. The principles of classical appetitive conditioning can also be used. Delay of reward, like delay of punishment, retards learning. But the teacher cannot always administer material rewards—such as food—immediately after a desirable response occurs. However, by associating previously neutral stimuli with primary rewards, the teacher can condition to the previously neutral stimuli responses that are similar to the responses to the primary rewards. When previously neutral stimuli have acquired the capacity to function as rewards, they are called learned rewards or *secondary reinforcers*. In other words, a secondary reinforcer is a stimulus that has no intrinsic value, but through association with an intrinsically valuable stimulus it has an acquired value. Typical secondary reinforcers include money, gold stars, and praise.

In the use of classical aversive conditioning, threat was interpreted as a signal of impending punishment. In classical appetitive conditioning, the analogous stimulus would be a promise of impending primary reward. Thus, the most effective secondary reinforcer should be promise of later reward, provided that the promise is consistently fulfilled. There is evidence that such promises are more effective than grades and teacher approval (see Witryol, 1971). Though grades and teacher approval are also secondary reinforcers, they are not as effective as direct promises of later primary rewards.

Instrumental Conditioning

Instrumental conditioning has been extensively studied in humans up to the college age (about 20 years old) and has received some attention in middle and old age. However, let us look at another study of infants, this one an example of instrumental conditioning, to provide a sharper contrast with classical conditioning. As in the example of classical conditioning—the study by Lipsitt, Kaye, and Bosack (1966)—the instrumental conditioning study to be described deals with the sucking response.

In this experiment Seltzer (1968) studied the acquisition and extinction of high-amplitude sucking in 10-day-old infants. He defined high-amplitude sucking as being stronger than the majority of sucks observed in an initial phase in which no rewards were given. The reward in the conditioning phase was .1 cc of milk (about 1-½ drops). The rewards were administered on one of two schedules. In one schedule every response was rewarded. This is the standard *continuous reinforcement* schedule. In the other schedule, every fifth response was rewarded. This is an *intermittent reinforcement* schedule.

The sucking responses were recorded automatically by the device Seltzer used. A nipple was put in the infant's mouth, and the milk reward was given if the sucking responses were made. That is, the reward was contingent on the occurrence of the responses. In contrast, in the classical conditioning study by Lipsitt, Kaye, and Bosack, the reward was delivered at a fixed, predetermined time regardless of the infant's responses. The reward in classical conditioning is not contingent on the subject's responses, but instead it depends on the passage of a certain amount of time following the presentation of the conditioned stimulus.

In Seltzer's study, one group of infants was given continuous reinforcement training then intermittent reinforcement training, a second group was given intermittent then continuous reinforcement training, and a third group was given continuous reinforcement training throughout. Following training, an extinction phase was given, in which no responses were rewarded.

It is a well-established finding in work on instrumental conditioning that giving intermittent reinforcement makes it harder to extinguish the response. That is, rewarding some but not all responses increases the stability or resistance to extinction. In agreement with this general finding, Seltzer found the greatest resistance to extinction in the group whose last training before extinction was on the intermittent reinforcement schedule (i.e., the group given continuous then intermittent reinforcement). There was no difference in resistance to extinction in the two groups whose last training was on the continuous reinforcement schedule (i.e., the group given intermittent then continuous reinforcement and the group given continuous reinforcement throughout).

The study therefore demonstrated that "components of the sucking response, a response that is initially closely tied to an eliciting stimulus, are amenable to control by reinforcement schedules" (Siqueland, 1970, p. 114). That is, a response that is itself a respondent has operant components that can be modified by reward contingencies. This finding is of theoretical significance because it casts some doubt on the operant-respondent distinction.

In addition, the study demonstrated that intermittent reinforcement affects the behavior of young infants, specifically the resistance to extinction of the behavior, in the same way that it has been shown in other research to affect the behavior of older children and animals. This finding is important because it shows that the principles of learning for young infants are similar to some of the principles for older children and animals. It shows, in other words, that there are similarities in learning processes across ages and across species. The theoretical significance of this finding is that it becomes possible to compare the course of learning across ages or species and to be able to infer differences in the way the causal variables operate.

Instrumental contingencies. In instrumental conditioning a stimulus that is absent before the response occurs is presented after the response occurs, or, alternatively, a stimulus that is present before the response occurs is terminated after the response. The presentation and withdrawal contingencies may increase or decrease the rate of the response. As shown in Table 2.1, these two variables —presentation versus withdrawal and increase versus decrease in response rate—define four types of contingent stimulus. (1) If *presenting* the stimulus after the response leads to an *increase* in the rate of the response, the stimulus is called a *positive reinforcer*. (2) If *presenting* the stimulus after the response leads to a *decrease* in the rate of the response, the stimulus is called a *punisher*. (3) If *withdrawing* the stimulus results in an *increase* in the rate of the response, the stimulus is called a *negative reinforcer*. Finally, (4) if *withdrawing* the stimulus results in a *decrease* in the rate of the response, the stimulus is called a *response cost* (Baer & Sherman, 1970).

You can see that the four kinds of stimulus are defined entirely in terms of what happens after the response —presentation or withdrawal—and what happens to the rate of the response—increase or decrease. One implication is that it is not necessarily true that a positive reinforcer can also be used as a response cost, nor that a punisher can be used as a negative reinforcer. However, research has shown that many positive reinforcers can in fact be used as response costs, and many punishers can be used as negative reinforcers.

Another implication of these definitions is that positive reinforcers and response costs are not necessarily appetitive stimuli and negative reinforcers and punishers are not necessarily aversive stimuli. Appetitive and aversive stimuli are defined by their hedonic values of pleasure or pain. The definitions of the four kinds of stimuli in Table 2.1 do not refer to hedonic value but only to consequences of presenta-

Table 2.1
Types of Contingent Stimuli Used in
Instrumental Conditioning

Contingency following the response	Consequent change in response rate	
	Increase	Decrease
Stimulus presented	Positive reinforcer	Punisher
Stimulus withdrawn	Negative reinforcer	Response cost

tion and withdrawal. However, research has shown that positive reinforcers and response costs are often appetitive stimuli, and negative reinforcers and punishers are often aversive stimuli.

The implication is that the teacher should be wary of making prior conclusions about the way contingent stimuli will work. The teacher may select a stimulus he thinks is appetitive and present it contingently upon some response. He may find, however, that instead of an increase in response rate, there will be no change. In such cases, he can conclude that the stimulus was not in fact a positive reinforcer.

A more serious mistake occurs when the contingent presentation of the stimulus results in a decrease in the response rate. In that case, the supposed positive reinforcer has turned out to be a punisher. For example, praise is generally expected to be positive in hedonic value, and therefore it should serve as a positive reinforcer when presented following a response. However, researchers who work with young children have often reported informally that after many repetitions the praise may change from a positive reinforcer to a punisher. The child reaches a point when he begins to say "Don't say 'Good!' anymore" and begins to reduce his response rate as though to avoid hearing the word of praise.

These considerations lead to a qualification that must be put on the conclusions suggested in the section on classical conditioning. Specifically, although it is expected that providing training by classical conditioning will make promises and threats effective as positive reinforcers and punishers, respectively, there may be individual children for whom the training will be ineffective. Maybe these children had home experiences in which promises and threats were not fulfilled. In any case, for these children the teacher must search for alternative reinforcers and punishers.

Classroom applications. The principles of instrumental conditioning are much more useful for everyday classroom teaching than are the principles of classical conditioning, because almost all classroom teaching deals with operant rather than respondent behaviors. In fact, it seems likely that the only utility of classical conditioning for the teacher is in the conditioning of emotional behaviors discussed earlier.

Of the many principles of instrumental conditioning that have classroom implications, we will cover only four. Of these four the principle of immediately presenting or withdrawing the contingent stimulus following the response has already been discussed. The others are related to intermittent reinforcement, avoidance conditioning, and *instructional praise*.

Intermittent schedules. The presentation or withdrawal of a stimulus need not occur every time the response occurs. When every response is followed by the contingency, the schedule of the contingency is continuous; and when some but not all of the responses are followed by the contingency, the schedule is intermittent. An intermittent schedule can be very lean, in the sense that only a few of the responses are followed by the contingency. If the schedule is too lean, extinction occurs. However, it is sometimes possible to maintain the response on a lean schedule by starting with a continuous schedule or an intermittent schedule with contingencies for most of the responses, and gradually reducing the number of responses for which consequences are presented.

The use of an intermittent schedule of contingencies has two advantages. First, if the rate of the response is high, the teacher will find it physically impossible to use a continuous schedule. The deliberate use of an intermittent schedule avoids this problem. Second, the use of an intermittent schedule is known to increase resistance to extinction. That is, when a response has been learned under an intermittent schedule, omission of all further contingencies will not eliminate the response as rapidly as when the response was learned under a continuous schedule. Therefore, if you want a response to occur even when the contingencies are no longer available, you should use an intermittent schedule in training. In contrast, if you want a response to disappear when the contingencies are no longer used, the response should be trained with a continuous schedule. However, even after training with a lean intermittent schedule, the response eventually will disappear unless the contingencies are reinstated. Thus, if the teacher responds to some but not all occurrences of a response, the rate of the response will be increased (conditioning) and will be maintained indefinitely if the contingency is reintroduced occasionally.

Avoidance conditioning. The third principle also involves resistance to extinction, but in this case, the conditioning situation is instrumental avoidance. In this procedure a signal is presented, followed by aversive stimulation unless the subject emits a response selected by the researcher. By making the response, the subject can avoid the aversive stimulus altogether. The principle is that instrumental avoidance training produces tremendous resistance to extinction. The reason is that after successful instrumental avoidance training, the subject responds to every presentation of the warning signal, and therefore never receives the aversive stimulus. During extinction, though the aversive stimulus is no longer presented, the subject never learns this because he never waits to find out.

Avoidance training has been assumed to underlie neurotic behavior, especially obsessive—compulsive behavior. The organism continues to perform a response that once functionally avoided aversive stimulation but is now functionless because the aversive stimulation would no longer be presented if the response failed to occur.

It is not entirely correct, however, to assert that avoidance behavior is functionless. If the behavior served no function, it would not occur. The problem, then, is to identify the function it serves, or, in other words, to identify the contingent stimulus that is maintaining the response during extinction.

Theoretical analysis of the conditioning situation solves the problem. First, in instrumental avoidance conditioning, a signal is presented and is followed by an aversive stimulus. After a number of training trials the appropriate response occurs and prevents the occurrence of the aversive stimulus. Subsequently, the rate of the response to the signal increases until the organism is consistently avoiding the aversive stimulus. At that point avoidance conditioning is complete. Let us analyze this conditioning situation further by looking again at the initial trials.

A signal is presented, followed by an aversive stimulus. The latter stimulus, being aversive, will be an eliciting stimulus for unconditioned responses including fear. With respect to these responses, the instrumental avoidance situation is actually a classical aversive conditioning situation. Consequently, the fear response (and possibly other components of the unconditioned response) should become conditioned to the signal. That is, the organism in the instrumental avoidance situation should come to fear the warning signal. In the instrumental avoidance situation the warning signal is terminated after the instrumental response occurs. The signal produced the fear and therefore terminating it reduces the fear. Thus, associated with the presentation of the signal is the occurrence of fear, and associated with the termination of the signal is the reduction of fear. The termination of the signal, and the consequent reduction of fear, fits the definition of the negative reinforcement contingency (Table 2.1).

Thus it appears that an aversive state, fear, is reduced following occurrence of the instrumental response. The instrumental response is therefore maintained by this negative reinforcement contingency. But late in training the organism is reliably avoiding presentation of the original aversive stimulus. Why, then, is there no extinction of the fear response to the signal? Apparently, the fear response is also maintained by the same negative reinforcement contingency. Presenting the signal arouses fear, and the fear response is followed by reduction of fear (when the signal is terminated following the occurrence of the instrumental response).

It follows that avoidance conditioning procedures should be used only when you want to train a response that will be extremely resistant to extinction.

Instructional praise.   The fourth principle of instrumental conditioning involves *instructional praise*. It has already been mentioned that praise can be an effective positive reinforcer. It has been found that instructional praise can be even more effective. Instructional praise means that the subject is not only praised, but he is also told explicitly why he is being praised. In telling the subject why he is being praised, it is necessary to be concrete. That is, the instructional part must refer to specific behavior and not to abstractions. For example, imagine that you are teaching a child the correct past tenses of irregular verbs. Suppose that before training, his past tenses were of the form "'wented," "goed," "taked," and the like (these forms are not unusual in young children). Let us assume that you choose to apply the training to his spontaneous speech. Thus you would praise him whenever he spontaneously said the correct form. However, he may not know why he is being praised. Therefore, you could give him instructions along with the praise. Suppose he usually says "I wented..." but one day you hear him say, "I went...." If your instructional praise is, "Very good; you used the correct past tense," it is not likely to be any more effective than praise alone. "Very good; you said 'went' " should be more effective than praise alone.

It is important to note that instruction alone, without praise, is often less effective than praise alone. That is, instruction works best when it is used to supplement praise as a positive reinforcer. This fact should not be surprising, because it is well known to parents and teachers that instructing a child how he ought to behave is often ineffective. Exhortations to behave do not work well. Similarly, instructing a person to use the typewriter by hitting Q, A, and Z with the little finger of the left hand, W, S, and X with the ring finger of the left hand, etc., will not teach him to be a typist. The instruction can eventually produce the desired effect only if coupled with practice and reinforcement.

Some researchers believe that the effectiveness of instructional praise results from the intervention of cognition. According to this interpretation, making the contingencies explicit by stating them makes it easier for the subject to be aware of these contingencies. If the contingent stimulus is powerful, the subject will probably choose to act in accord with it. However, he can also—according to this interpretation —choose not to act in accord with the contingency. Thus, instrumental conditioning, like classical conditioning, can be interpreted as being influenced by cognitive processes. Also, as with classical conditioning, instrumental conditioning can influence cognitive processes. Here again, there are psychotherapeutic techniques based on the instrumental conditioning of cognitions (e.g., Cautela, 1971). A person can control his own thoughts, images, and urges by imposing on them an imagined contingent stimulus. For example, if you imagine an unpleasant scene whenever you have the urge to smoke, you punish the occurrence of the urge, helping you to give up smoking.

Summary of Conditioning

Classical conditioning. In classical conditioning a neutral stimulus (the conditioned stimulus) is presented and is followed by another stimulus (the unconditioned stimulus) which arouses some response of interest (the unconditioned response). After many paired presentations of these two stimuli, the conditioned stimulus acquires the capacity to arouse the response (conditioned response). The unconditioned stimulus can be appetitive—a stimulus that is normally sought by the organism—or it can be aversive—a stimulus normally avoided by the organism. When appetitive stimuli are used, the conditioned response may include positive emotions. When aversive stimuli are used, the conditioned response may include fear or other negative emotions. Thus, as a result of conditioning, stimuli associated with appetitive stimuli may come to arouse pleasurable expectations, and stimuli associated with aversive stimuli may come to arouse fear. Classical conditioning is possible in early infancy, and may have more general utility at that age than at later ages, except in the conditioning of emotional responses and in psychotherapy.

Instrumental conditioning. In instrumental conditioning the subject controls the presentation or withdrawal of a stimulus by his own responses. The stimulus is presented or withdrawn, depending on the schedule, only if the subject emits the appropriate behavior. The stimulus that is contingent on the subject's responses is usually categorized according to the effect it has on the responses. The categories are positive reinforcer (presentation following the response increases the rate of the response); punisher (presentation decreases response rate); negative reinforcer (withdrawal increases response rate); and response cost (withdrawal decreases response rate). It is not always possible to tell ahead of time how a stimulus should be categorized.

Unlike classical conditioning, instrumental conditioning has many practical applications. However, since delaying the presentation or withdrawal of the contingent stimulus will retard learning, the stimulus should be presented or withdrawn immediately after the response occurs.

It is not necessary to impose the contingency following every response. Intermittent schedules of imposing the contingency can lead to conditioning, and, in addition, they can increase the resistance to extinction of the conditioned response. Even after intermittent reinforcement, however, extinction will eventually occur if no more reinforcers are given.

Instrumental avoidance training, in which the subject learns to respond to a signal and thereby to avoid aversive stimulation, produces tremendous resistance to extinction. Such training should therefore be used only if resistance to extinction is desirable.

Instructional praise is a form of positive reinforcement in which the reinforcer is accompanied by an explicit statement about why the reinforcer is being given. It is generally more effective than instruction alone and is often more effective than praise alone.

Instrumental conditioning, like classical conditioning, can apparently be influenced by cognitive processes. In addition, both kinds of conditioning seem to be capable of influencing cognitive processes.

Suggested Readings

Classical Conditioning

Siqueland, E. R. Basic learning processes: I. Classical conditioning. In H. W. Reese & L. P. Lipsitt (Eds.), *Experimental child psychology*. New York: Academic Press, 1970.

Instrumental Conditioning

Bijou, S. W., & Ribes-Inesta, E. (Eds.), *Behavior modification: Issues and extensions*. New York: Academic Press, 1972.

Hulsebus, R. C. Operant conditioning of infant behavior: A review. In H. W. Reese (Ed.), *Advances in child development and behavior*. Vol. 8. New York: Academic Press, 1973.

Siqueland, E. R., & Ryan, T. J. Basic learning processes: II. Instrumental conditioning. In H. W. Reese & L. P. Lipsitt (Eds.), *Experimental child psychology*. New York: Academic Press, 1970.

General

Stevenson, H. W. Learning in children. In P. H. Mussen (Ed.), *Carmichael's manual of child psychology*. (3rd ed.) Vol. I. New York: Wiley, 1970.

Chapter 3 Discriminative Learning

Discriminative learning, or discrimination learning, refers to a variety of situations in which a person (or animal) must learn to respond selectively. In perhaps the simplest discriminative-learning task, the subject must learn to choose one of two objects consistently and learn not to choose the other object. To achieve this, the experimenter shows the subject two objects, usually side by side, and allows him to make a choice. Typically, only one choice is permitted on each presentation of the two objects. That is, if the subject chooses correctly, he is given a reward of some kind—either a material reward, such as a small piece of candy or cereal, or verbal praise. If he chooses incorrectly, he is not rewarded and must wait until the next presentation before being given the opportunity to choose the other object. Each presentation constitutes a separate training trial. Training usually continues until the subject is consistently choosing the correct object. The correct object is arbitrarily designated the correct one by the experimenter. It is also called the *positive* stimulus, and the incorrect object is the *negative* stimulus. Discriminative-learning problems may include several negative stimuli.

Some Background Information

Purpose. The experimenter's goal in studying discriminative learning is to determine how organisms learn to respond selectively and, beyond that, to determine what variables aid or retard this type of learning. Many students find it difficult to understand why anyone would be interested in studying discriminative learning. The task, with its repeated presentations of two objects, seems far removed from any kind of learning that goes on in the real world outside the psychological laboratory. However, as we will see later in this chapter, what has been learned so far about discriminative learning does have some practical implications.

Sample study. An example of discriminative learning by children is part of a study by Reese (1962a). (The other part of this study is discussed in the following chapter.) Reese trained children on a discriminative-learning problem in which three stimuli were presented. The stimuli were wooden blocks that differed in size. The subject had to learn to choose the middle-sized block. Whenever he made the correct choice, he received a reward. The rewards were animal and flower stickers, which the subject pasted on a sheet of paper. The positions of the blocks varied across trials, so that sometimes the middle-sized block was in the middle of the three-block array, and other times it was at the left or right end of the array.

The similarity of the sizes of the stimuli was varied in two conditions. In one condition the sizes were very similar (a 1.3 to 1 ratio of surface areas), and in the other the sizes were obviously different (a 2 to 1 ratio of surface areas). The subjects were five- and six-year-olds. Half of each age group was given the problem with the similar sizes, and the other half was given the problem with the distinctive sizes.

The results of the study are summarized in Table 3.1. Statistical analysis showed that the similarity of the stimuli affected the difficulty of the problem, especially for the younger children. Discrimination with similar stimuli was considerably harder for the younger children to solve than was discrimination with distinctive stimuli. For the older children the difference in difficulty was negligible. In addition, on the difficult problem the younger children were considerably worse than the older children, but on the easy problem the younger children were as good as the older children.

These findings illustrate the effects of two variables that have often been found to influence discriminative learning: age of subjects and similarity of stimuli. We will look at these and other variables that influence discriminative learning in the rest of this chapter. The variables are organized into three classes: (1) subject characteristics, including age and IQ, motivation, and attention; (2) task characteristics, including stimulus similarity and others; and (3) procedural variables, including *shaping* and *fading*.

Table 3.1

Average Number of Trials Required to Solve Discriminative Problems in Reese (1962a) Study

	Problem	
Age Group	*Similar Stimuli*	*Distinctive Stimuli*
5 years	23.8	10.0
6 years	13.9	10.2

After Reese, H. W. The distance effect in transposition in the intermediate size problem. *Journal of Comparative and Physiological Psychology,* 1962a, 55, Table 1, p. 529. Copyright 1962 by the American Psychological Association. Used by permission.

Subject Characteristics

Age and IQ. It has been found that age and IQ affect the speed of discriminative learning in the same way. For this reason we will discuss these two variables together.

Older children and children with higher IQs tend to learn faster than younger children (preschool and kindergarten) and children with lower IQs. However, the effects of age and IQ are not strong. This conclusion is demonstrated by the relatively wide spans of age and IQ that must be examined before large differences in learning are found.

In general, the reason children who are either young or low in IQ do less well on a discriminative-learning task is that they tend to respond to the positions of the objects rather than to the objects themselves. They tend to choose whichever object is on the left, for example, or to alternate between the positions, choosing the left object, then the right, then left, etc. These position habits, referred to as position preference and position alternation, are also found in older children, but older children abandon them much more promptly than younger children do. The reason for this age difference may be that younger children (and children with low IQs) are more willing to settle for intermittent rewards.

In a standard discriminative-learning experiment the position of the correct object is changed at random from trial to trial. For example, in the first ten trials the positions of the correct object might be those shown in Table 3.2. Each row in the table shows the trials on which the subject would be right and wrong if he was using a particular position habit or the correct solution (last row). You can see that all of the position habits yield a reward by chance on about half the trials. This frequency of chance reward is obtained by design. The series of left-right positions given in the table is from a series constructed by Gellermann (1933) specifically to yield 50 percent reward from position habits. The older child, however, will usually not be satisfied to receive rewards only half the time, and therefore, if he started out with a position habit, he will likely abandon it to try out some other solution. The

Table 3.2
Effect of Position Habits on Frequency of Reward

Item	Trial 1	2	3	4	5	6	7	8	9	10	Percentage Reward
Position of Correct Object	R	R	R	L	L	R	L	R	L	L	
Left Preference	−	−	−	+	+	−	+	−	+	+	50
Right Preference	+	+	+	−	−	+	−	+	−	−	50
Alternation (LR)	−	+	−	−	+	+	+	+	+	−	60
Alternation (RL)	+	−	+	+	−	−	−	−	−	+	40
Double Alternation (LLRR)	−	−	+	−	+	−	−	+	+	+	50
Double Alternation (RRLL)	+	+	−	+	−	+	+	−	−	−	50
Problem Solution	+	+	+	+	+	+	+	+	+	+	100

Note: + means correct choice; − means incorrect choice.

younger child, in contrast, may well be satisfied with 50 percent reward. It is, after all, better than no reward at all, and for all the child knows any other solution might be completely wrong. The young child seems to believe that a solution that yields rewards half the time must be at least partially correct. Even so, he will eventually notice that the reward is correlated with the objects and not their positions, and this realization will enable him to solve the problem.

In some experiments older children (for example, fifth graders) have been superior to college students in the speed of discriminative learning. The reason is that for the college student the solution to the problem is unbelieveably simple. Confronted with a discrimination problem involving two objects differing in size, for example, the college student may immediately recognize the possibility that one size is always correct and the other always incorrect, but he may reason that if that is the correct solution, the study is trivial. Therefore, he searches for a more complex solution that would tax his reasoning powers. While he is trying out these complex solutions, he is making errors, of course, and as a result he may take more trials to find the correct solution than a fifth-grader. The fifth-grader is not astounded by learning tasks that present no intellectual challenge, and consequently he is willing to try out the very simple solution that turns out to be correct.

Age and the role of errors.   Related to the effects of age on discriminative learning is a belief that the older child and adult are surprised when they are wrong, and the younger child is surprised when he is correct. If so, then errors would be more important to older children and adults and rewarded responses should be more important to younger children. You should be aware, however, that in discriminative learning, the correct solution to the problem produces only correct responses. In other words, the correct solution cannot yield errors. Therefore, the occurrence of an error is a reliable indication that the solution being attempted is wrong. Consequently, the older child and adult, who presumably are attending to errors, should quickly abandon incorrect solutions as soon as they produce errors, as they inevitably must.

In contrast, rewarded responses can be produced by incorrect solutions. As shown in Table 3.2, any of the position habits can produce rewarded responses on about half the trials. Therefore, the occurrence of a rewarded response does not reliably indicate that the attempted solution is correct. However, if the young child is attending to rewarded responses, he is paying little attention to errors. Because errors are the only reliable indicators that an attempted solution is wrong, the young child will require more training to learn that a wrong solution is wrong.

You should keep in mind that this discussion about the relationship between age and the role of errors in discriminative learning is highly speculative. First, there is no *direct* evidence that errors become more important in discriminative learning as a child's age increases. Second, there is some evidence from another kind of study that errors are more important than correct responses for both younger and older children. However, this evidence is indirect because it comes from a different kind of learning situation (*learning set*, discussed in Chapter 4).

Motivation.   Another characteristic of subjects that affects performance in the discriminative-learning task is motivation. Motivation in the psychology of human behavior is a very complicated topic. In animals there are a few basic motives, such as hunger, thirst, and sex, that result from depriving the animal of a substance or activity needed for the individual's or species' survival. In addition, animals seem to have a motive that might be called curiosity, which theoretically is also related to deprivation. Curiosity, according to theory, results from a lack of variety in the stimulus environment.

Most human behavior is obviously not motivated by the basic needs required for survival. The human being has a vast array of motives, which, it is assumed, are learned rather than innate. Even curiosity in the human being seems to have a learned component. It is generally believed that these learned motives, or *secondary drives*, are the major sources of motivation for human behavior. That they can vary in strength from person to person or in one person from occasion to occasion helps to explain the great variety of human behavior.

There are optimal levels of motivation. Below the optimum, performance is impaired because the person is not sufficiently motivated to perform well. Above the optimum, performance is also impaired because the person is so strongly motivated that he is distracted from the task requirements.

These effects of motivational level can be explained theoretically, but the theory is rather complicated and will not be discussed here (see Longstreth, 1968, pp. 215-217, for a minimally technical discussion). What the theoretical analysis shows is that a well-learned response tendency will be strengthened by increased motivation relatively more than a less well-learned response tendency will. Therefore, if the well-learned tendency is correct, increased motivation improves performance; but if the well-learned tendency is incorrect, increased motivation impairs performance. The optimal level of motivation consequently depends upon the subject's prior learning and the nature of the task requirements.

In discriminative-learning tasks, the experimenter often selects as the response to be rewarded one that is relatively weak in the subject's hierarchy of response tendencies. Otherwise, learning would be too fast to be psychologically interesting. Therefore, a high level of motivation generally impairs performance in a discriminative-learning study. However, once the problem has been solved, the correct response will be the strongest in the hierarchy, and then higher motivation will further improve performance. In short, a moderate level of motivation is best if the material is new, and a high level of motivation is best if the material is already known.

Attention theory. One final subject characteristic to be considered here is attention. Attention is a kind of screening device by which certain aspects of a situation are scrutinized and other aspects are ignored. Attention, then, is selective. In discriminative-learning situations, a subject who attends to irrelevant aspects of the setting, such as position of the objects, will not be attending to the relevant aspect, the nature of the difference between the objects. It has been theorized that the course of discriminative learning is separated into two successive stages. In the first stage the subject learns what to attend to. That is, he learns which of the objects' various dimensions are relevant to the discrimination. In the second stage he learns which specific values on these dimensions are associated with reward. Thus, the subject learns first what to look at and then what to choose.

Table 3.3 shows a discrimination problem in which color is the relevant dimension; and position, size, and shape are irrelevant. Two stimuli are presented on each trial, and each stimulus has a value on all four dimensions: color (red or blue), position (on left or right side), size (large or small), and shape (square or triangle). Different types of settings are used on different trials, in a random sequence. Thus, for example, in the first setting type in Table 3.3 the two combinations of dimensional values that are presented are a large red square to the left of a small blue triangle. If the subject chooses the large red square, in this example, he receives a reward and if he chooses the small blue triangle he receives no reward.

Table 3.4 shows which values on the dimensions are rewarded and nonrewarded in each setting type. Note that responses to all values of the irrelevant dimensions (left-right, large-small, square-triangle) are rewarded half the time, on the average. Furthermore, one value on the relevant dimension (red in the example) is always associated with reward and the other value (blue) is never associated with reward.

In the first stage of discriminative learning, in this example, the subject learns to attend to color and not to attend to

---

Table 3.3
Sample Discrimination Problem with Color Relevant and Position, Size, and Shape Irrelevant

| Setting | Positions of Stimuli | |
Type	Left	Right
1	Large red square (+)	Small blue triangle (−)
1′	Small blue triangle (−)	Large red square (+)
2	Small red square (+)	Large blue triangle (−)
2′	Large blue triangle (−)	Small red square (+)
3	Large red triangle (+)	Small blue square (−)
3′	Small blue square (−)	Large red triangle (+)
4	Small red triangle (+)	Large blue square (−)
4′	Large blue square (−)	Small red triangle (+)

Note: + and − indicate whether choice of the stimulus is rewarded or nonrewarded, respectively. A "setting type" includes both stimuli in the row. The setting types with a primed number are identical to the setting types with the corresponding unprimed number except for the positions of the two stimuli.

Table 3.4
Reward and Nonreward of Dimensional Values in the
Sample Discrimination Problem in Table 3.3

	Dimension							
Setting	Color		Position		Size		Shape	
Type	Red	Blue	Left	Right	Large	Small	Square	Triangle
1	+	−	+	−	+	−	+	−
1′	+	−	−	+	+	−	+	−
2	+	−	+	−	−	+	+	−
2′	+	−	−	+	−	+	+	−
3	+	−	+	−	+	−	−	+
3′	+	−	−	+	+	−	−	+
4	+	−	+	−	−	+	−	+
4′	+	−	−	+	−	+	−	+
Overall Percent	100	0	50	50	50	50	50	50

position, size, and shape. In the second stage he learns that red is the color associated with reward. Thus, according to this theory of the role of attention in discriminative learning, the subject learns first what is relevant and then what is correct.

Attention research. The research on which the attention theory of discriminative learning is based has shown, among other things, that mental retardation is associated with a slowness of learning only in the first stage. Mentally retarded subjects require longer to learn what is relevant, but once they have solved this first-stage problem, they exhibit no retardation in the second stage. After learning what is relevant, they learn what is correct as rapidly as children with normal intelligence. This finding has important implications about the nature of mental retardation. Perhaps the most important is that deficits in learning in mentally retarded children result largely from deficits in attentional processes rather than from deficits in learning ability per se.

The research is also important for its implications about

Table 3.5
Salience of Stimulus Dimensions for Young Children

Dimension	Preschoolers	Kindergarteners
Color	1	2
Number	2	3.5
Size	3	3.5
Form	4	1

Note: 1 = most salient. Based on data reported by Lee (1965).

learning in normal children. For example, increasing the *salience* of the relevant dimension should promote learning in the first stage. The salience of a dimension is the likelihood that it will be attended to. Thus, a salient dimension is one that a subject is likely to look at. Some dimensions are intrinsically more salient than others; some are more likely than others to grab a child's attention. However, it has been found that the ordering of salience varies with age. As shown in Table 3.5, color is most salient for preschoolers, then number, then size, then form. For kindergarteners, form is most salient, color is next, then number and size are tied for least salient. Form is also most salient for older children. The ordering can be changed, however, by varying the similarity of the values selected to represent the dimensions. For example, with very similar colors and more markedly different sizes, size becomes more salient than color.

The salience of a dimension can be increased by making the values optimally different, that is, by making the values different enough but not too different. Theoretically, a dimension is not perceived as a dimension unless there are simultaneously present at least two values on the dimension. Thus, if two values are exceedingly similar to one another, for example two very similar shades of blue, the subject may fail to observe that color is a possible dimension. Conversely, if the values are exceedingly far apart on the dimension, the subject may fail to observe the dimension. For example, pinheads and cartwheels may be so different in size that the size dimension is not noticed. Similarly, the sounds of crickets and sixteen-inch guns may be so different in loudness that the loudness dimension is not noticed (Koffka, 1922; Lashley, 1938). Unfortunately, however, although it is possible to specify differences that are so small or so large that the dimension involved is hard to detect, the optimal range of differences has never been established by research with children. We do know, though, that it must be close to the middle range of possible differences.

Another way to speed up the first stage of discriminative learning is to reduce the number of irrelevant dimensions. This procedure should be easier to accomplish than increasing the salience of the dimensions. For example, if you wanted to teach children to discriminate colors, you would need to include some discriminations between similar shades. Because of the similarity of the colors in these discriminations, color would not be a salient dimension unless you eliminated differences on irrelevant dimensions. You should therefore use objects that differ only in color.

Another way to reduce the number of irrelevant dimensions is to increase the number of relevant dimensions. For example, suppose the objects differ in color, size, and shape: red or green, large or small, and square or triangle. If color is the only relevant dimension—choose all red objects regardless of size and shape—the discrimination is harder than if all three dimensions are relevant—choose any red, any large, or any square. Knowing which dimensions are salient and knowing how to control salience can be put to practical use. One application is discussed under *Transposition* in Chapter 4.

Task Characteristics

There are several task characteristics that affect the speed of discriminative learning. We will examine four of these: (1) the similarity of the objects to be discriminated, (2) separation between the objects, (3) separation of the objects from the place for responding, and (4) the nature of the objects.

Stimulus similarity. It should be intuitively obvious that learning to discriminate between two objects that are similar to one another is more difficult than learning to discriminate between two objects that are distinctively different. The research evidence confirms that this is the case. However, the research has not dealt with the extreme differences mentioned in the previous section (pinheads and cartwheels; crickets and sixteen-inch guns), and it is likely that learning would be impaired with such large discrepancies between objects.

Separation between stimuli. Within the range of stimulus similarity that has been studied, it has been found that the distance between the stimuli influences the difficulty of the discrimination. When the stimuli are far apart, the discrimination is more difficult than when they are close together. In fact, a discrimination between two widely separated objects that are moderately distinctive is harder than a discrimination between two stimuli that are more similar but close together. The usual explanation is that reducing the amount of separation between the stimuli makes the stimuli easier to compare. There is extensive evidence (see review by Reese, 1968) that comparison is associated with successful discrimination, not only in human subjects but also in other mammals including sea lions and porpoises. It is interesting that pharmacists seem to have learned from experience that separation and similarity interact in this way. The usual rule in a pharmacy is to place drugs that are similar in appearance next to each other on the shelf. The explanation the pharmacists give for this practice is that it forces them to read the labels in order to make a choice.

Separation between stimulus and response locations. A third task characteristic that affects discriminative learning is the separation between the place where the stimuli are presented and the place where responses are made. For example, in the apparatus diagrammed in Figure 3.1 the stimulus locations are separated from the response locations. The subject must look in one

Figure 3.1

Diagrammatic representation of an apparatus for studying discriminative learning. The front is viewed by the subject; the experimenter generally sits behind the apparatus to manipulate the controls. The circles labeled S_1 and S_2 are windows in which the stimuli are shown. The circles labeled R_1 and R_2 are push buttons which the subject pushes to indicate which stimulus he is choosing. Note that the location of a stimulus is some distance away from the location of the response which indicates choice of that stimulus.

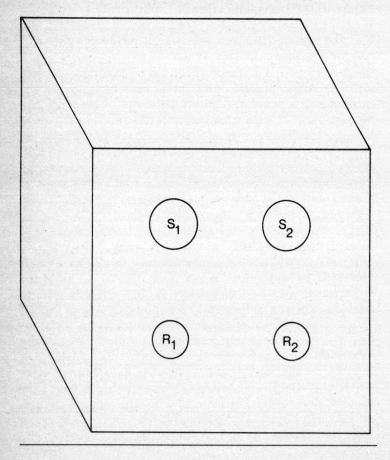

place to see a stimulus (S_1 or S_2 in the diagram), and must look below it to see the push button (R_1 or R_2 in the diagram). If the apparatus were modified by eliminating the push buttons and the subject were required to touch one of the stimuli to indicate his choice, there would be no separation between the stimulus and response locations.

When the locations of the stimuli and responses are separated, the discrimination is harder. The reason appears to be related to the salience of the position dimension. In a problem requiring discrimination between stimulus objects, the positions of the objects are irrelevant. The correct object appears equally often on the left and right. It follows that anything that emphasizes the positions, or makes position a more salient cue, should make the discrimination harder. When there is no separation between the stimulus and response locations—that is, when the subject responds directly to the stimulus—the position of the stimulus is likely not to be noticed because the last thing the subject sees while making a response is the stimulus itself. However, when the response is to a different location from the location of the stimulus, the last thing the subject sees is the response unit. Because the response units are identical except for being in different positions, position becomes the last cue seen when the response is made, and consequently position becomes a more salient cue.

This theoretical interpretation of the effect of separation between stimulus and response locations is supported by studies of the effects of increasing the salience of the positions. In these studies, cues that are irrelevant to the discrimination are confounded with the positions. For example, in one study (Shepp, 1962) there was no separation between the stimulus and response locations. Position should therefore not have been a salient cue. However, for one group different rewards were given for correct responses in the different positions. Miniature marshmallows were given for correct responses when the positive stimulus was on the left, and small chocolates were given for correct responses when the positive stimulus was on the right. (Using good experimental procedure, Shepp reversed these associations for half of the group, giving marshmallows for the right and chocolates for the left.) For another group, the marshmallows and chocolates were also used as rewards, together with candy corn and other candies, but none of the candies was associated systematically with any one position. A third group received only one kind of candy as a reward. Thus, in the first group positions were associated with different kinds of candies, and in the other two groups position was not associated with type of reward. As expected, learning was retarded in the first group. Increasing the salience of the positions by associating each with a different kind of reward made the discrimination harder.

Nature of stimuli. The last task characteristic we will consider is the nature of the stimuli. Stimuli can be *planometric* or *stereometric*. Planometric stimuli vary in width and depth; stereometric stimuli vary in width, depth, and height. In addition, both kinds of stimuli can vary on other dimensions, such as shape and color. Thus the distinguishing characteristic is height: planometric stimuli are flat, and stereometric stimuli are not.

It has been found that both monkeys and children learn discriminations between stereometric stimuli more easily than they learn discriminations between planometric stimuli (Reese, 1963, 1964). In fact, discrimination is easiest when the stereometric stimuli are "junk" objects, constructed literally of junk. Scraps of wood, metal, cloth, and so forth are combined haphazardly to make the objects, and consequently the objects differ on many dimensions—size, shape, color, texture, weight, complexity, familiarity, and so on. In addition, many of the dimensions are relevant. Since the discrimination problem could be solved by attending to any one of the many relevant dimensions, the subject is more likely to be attending to a relevant dimension early in the problem than he is when there are only a few relevant dimensions. There are usually more relevant dimensions in stereometric stimuli than in planometric stimuli, which explains the greater ease of learning discriminations between stereometric stimuli.

Procedural Variables

Another class of variables affecting discriminative learning includes procedural variables. We will discuss two of the most effective of these variables here. The first, *shaping*, is a procedure by which the response of the subject is changed until it has the desired topography. The second, *fading*, is a procedure by which the stimulus that controls the response is changed until it has the desired characteristics. These procedures will become clear later. At this point you need only keep in mind that shaping is applied to responses and fading is applied to stimuli.

Purpose of shaping.   Shaping is used when the subject does not emit the desired response. In the discrimination situation, the desired response is the choice of the positive stimulus. However, the subject cannot learn this response if he never approaches the response locations. Shaping can be used to get the subject to approach the response locations. Once this has been achieved, discriminative training can be used to get the subject to choose the positive object by approaching the response location associated with that object. In the shaping procedure, then, the goal is to get the subject to emit the discriminative response, that is, the response to the locations where responses are supposed to be made.

Verbal and nonverbal shaping.   A very simple kind of shaping is found in studies with children whose responses are shaped by instructions. For example, using an apparatus like the one diagrammed in Figure 3.1, the experimenter might turn on the stimulus lights (S_1 and S_2) and point to them and then to the push buttons (R_1 and R_2) while saying, "See these lights and these buttons? If you push the correct button, you will get a marble. The lights will tell you which button you should push." Spiker (1959) used instructions very much like these with preschoolers, and similar ones have been used in many other studies with preschoolers. The instructions were apparently successful in shaping the response to the push buttons, because one group in Spiker's study made more than

75 percent correct responses in the first six trials. Obviously, they could not respond *correctly* until they had learned how and where to make a response.

When the subjects are animals or preverbal children, instructions cannot be used for shaping the desired response. In a study with infants, Weisberg and Simmons (1966) used a shaping procedure to orient the infants to the task. In this study, there was no separation between the stimulus and response locations. The stimuli were objects presented on a tray, and the response was pushing an object aside to reveal a small hole that could contain the reward. The reward, candy or cookie, was hidden under the positive object. In the shaping procedure, the first step was to train the infant to pick up the reward from the tray. The candy or cookie was simply placed on the tray within the infant's reach, and the infant was encouraged to reach for it and take it. The objects were not presented at all during this first step. Second, the infant was trained to retrieve the reward from the small holes. This step was done by placing the reward in one of the small holes, with the stimulus objects behind the holes. Next, the second step was repeated with the stimulus objects half covering the holes, and finally the step was repeated with the stimulus objects completely covering the holes.

As you can see, during the first two steps the child learns to retrieve the reward, first from the tray and then from the small hole. During the last two steps, the child continues to use the retrieval response that he learned in the first two steps and learns how he is supposed to manipulate the stimulus objects in order to be able to make the retrieval response. In both cases shaping begins with a response that is not the same as the desired response, though it resembles it in some way. After the subject has learned to make this response, he is required to learn another response that is more like the desired response. This process of requiring closer and closer approximations to the desired response, until the desired response is actually being made, is characteristic of shaping procedures.

Size of steps in shaping. A practical problem in using the shaping procedure is the question of how small to make the transitions between steps. If the transitions are too large, shaping is impeded; and if the transitions are too small, shaping is unnecessarily slow. For example, suppose the subject is able to understand instructions. In this case, if instructions are given, shaping can occur in one large step. However, if instructions are not given but instead a nonverbal shaping procedure is used, as in the Weisberg and Simmons study, then shaping will proceed by small steps and will take longer than the instructions would have.

Nonverbal shaping necessarily proceeds by relatively small steps. Instructions almost always proceed by one large step, though they could proceed by small steps. If the required response is complex, then even a child who comprehends speech may need instructions that proceed by small steps. In such cases, it may be that nonverbal shaping would be more efficient. Unfortunately, there has been no study in which a comparison has been made between small-step instructions and nonverbal shaping. Therefore, we do not know which method would work better. However, in classroom applications, it seems obvious that small-step instructions would be easier to use than nonverbal shaping, because nonverbal shaping requires a one-to-one relationship between the teacher and the student while instructions can be given to the entire class.

In Chapter 2 we saw that instructions alone are generally not as effective as instructional praise. This observation seems to contradict the proposal that instructions can be used for shaping. However, two considerations make the proposal reasonable. First, the kind of instruction that is generally limited in effectiveness involves a single large step, rather than the sequence of small steps recommended here for shaping. The small-step instructions should be more effective, and therefore the recommended procedure should work. Second, researchers have found from experience that instructions are most effective when they are accompanied by a demonstration. There is even experimental evidence to back up this informal observation (Corsini, 1969). But the use of a demonstration implies segmented, relatively small-step instructions. Therefore, this observation increases our confidence that the recommended procedure will work.

Fading in. In the fading procedure, the stimuli are changed in small steps until the desired characteristics control responses. In the example that follows, the experimental procedure begins with shaping and then shifts to fading. In this case, the procedure involves fading *in* a stimulus. Fading *out* will be considered in the next section.

In a discrimination problem the experimenter might begin by presenting only the positive stimulus and rewarding the subject each time he makes the desired response to this stimulus. The response might be picking up the stimulus, and the reward, finding a marble or other token under the stimulus. Picking up the positive stimulus is the same as choosing the positive stimulus, provided there are other stimuli present that are not picked up (or chosen). Therefore, teaching the child to pick up the positive stimulus when it is presented alone can be a precursor to discriminative training in which the positive stimulus is presented with a negative stimulus. In the fading procedure, once the child is reliably approaching and picking up the positive stimulus when it is presented alone, the experimenter can gradually begin to present the negative stimulus.

Let us examine these procedures in detail. Suppose the two stimuli will be presented on a tray, with each stimulus covering a small hole that can contain the reward. The experimenter might begin training by shaping the selective response, using the procedure already described. In the first step, no stimulus objects are presented. The reward is placed on the tray and the subject is allowed to retrieve it. Next, the reward is placed in one of the small holes, sometimes the one on the right and sometimes the one on the left, and the subject is again allowed to retrieve it. Thus far, the subject has learned several things. He has learned where the holes are located on the tray. He has learned that rewards are located in the holes, and that they can be located in either hole. Finally, he has learned that he is allowed to retrieve the reward when he sees it.

In the next step the object that is to be the positive stimulus in the discrimination phase is placed on the tray behind one of the holes, and the reward is placed in that hole. This step continues, with the object sometimes placed behind the hole on the right and sometimes behind the hole on the left. The subject learns in this phase that the hole with the object behind it is the one containing the reward.

Next, the object is moved forward so that half of the hole is covered, but the reward is still visible in the hole. In this step, the subject learns that the reward is in the hole associated with the object even when the reward is hard to see. In addition, he learns to push the object aside in order to retrieve the reward.

In the next step the object completely covers the hole. The subject should immediately shove the object aside, applying the learning of the previous step, and retrieve the reward. At this point an observer who had not seen the shaping procedure would report that the subject reliably responds to the stimulus object. The response made—shoving aside the object—is the same one that will later be required in the discrimination phase. Thus, the shaping process has been completed successfully and the experimenter can begin the fading procedure.

The purpose of the fading procedure is to introduce the negative stimulus without disrupting the subject's responses to the positive stimulus. To continue the above illustration, the experimenter can accomplish this by proceeding through steps similar to those used in shaping. Throughout the fading procedure, however, the positive stimulus continues to be presented, completely covering the reward.

The first step in the fading procedure is to present the negative stimulus in a position well behind the empty hole. The subject has already learned during the shaping procedure that rewards are found only in the holes, and he has also learned where the holes are located. Therefore, he should have no tendency to shove aside the negative stimulus and should continue to respond only to the positive stimulus.

Next, the negative stimulus is moved closer to the empty hole, and in successive small steps it is moved to cover half the hole and finally to cover it completely. The subject learns in these steps that this stimulus is always associated with an empty hole, and therefore he should continue to select only the positive stimulus. At this point, when both holes are completely covered by the stimulus objects and the subject is reliably choosing only the positive stimulus, the discrimination has been learned.

Fading out.   The other fading procedure involves fading *out* a stimulus. Here the experimenter uses a stimulus to control the response, but the stimulus is not the one that is desired to control the response. The two stimuli are presented simultaneously, and gradually the control is shifted to the desired stimulus by slowly removing the undesirable stimulus. For example, the two stimuli in a discrimination problem might be presented simultaneously, and the experimenter might touch the positive stimulus to indicate that the subject should pick up that one to find the reward. If the subject's response has been appropriately shaped, either by a nonverbal shaping procedure or by instructions to pick up the one touched by the experimenter, the subject will in fact pick up the correct stimulus. The response is controlled, however, not by the desired or positive stimulus, but rather by an undesired stimulus, the experimenter's touching. Gradually, the experimenter fades out his touching, perhaps first by changing from touching to pointing, and then by pointing in a more and more cursory and incomplete way. As the pointing is faded out, control will shift gradually to the positive stimulus, because it is systematically associated with reward. Finally, the pointing will be eliminated completely, and the positive stimulus will completely control the response.

Applications of shaping and fading.   If the steps in shaping and fading are gradual enough, a subject can solve a discrimination problem without ever making an error. Though this procedure may be laborious, it can also be extremely useful. It is most useful, of course, in situations in which an error would produce harmful consequences.

At this point you may be wondering if, in the shaping and fading procedure that produces discriminative learning without errors, the subject learns only about the positive consequences of choosing the positive stimulus and not about the negative consequences of choosing the negative stimulus. After all, how could the subject learn about these negative consequences if he never chooses the negative stimulus? It turns out, however, that during fading the subject actually does learn about the negative consequences without ever choosing the negative stimulus. Research has shown that even in the errorless-discrimination procedure, the negative stimulus acquires aversive properties, just as it would in the standard discriminative-learning procedure in which many errors typically occur.

Another application of fading procedures is in the use of prompts during the initial stages of teaching new concepts. Gradually, these prompts are made more superficial until they are eliminated entirely. The technique can be used with an entire class provided the steps are small enough for the slowest students. However, if the range of ability in the class is large, such small steps may create a boring situation for the more able students. Therefore, like many instructional techniques, fading procedures are most effective when the range of abilities in the class is relatively small.

Summary of Discriminative Learning

Discriminative learning means learning to respond selectively to stimuli. The speed of discriminative learning is influenced by many variables, including subject characteristics, task characteristics, and procedural variables.

Subject characteristics. The subject characteristics that affect discriminative learning include age and IQ, motivation, and attention.

Younger and lower-IQ children solve discriminative-learning problems more slowly than older and higher-IQ children. However, the effects of age and IQ are not striking, and large age-spans or IQ-ranges must be studied to find important differences in discriminative learning. It appears that position habits, which interfere with successful discriminative learning, are the source of the effects of age and IQ. Younger and lower-IQ children tend to have stronger position habits.

Human behavior is motivated more by learned motives than by primary motives such as hunger and thirst. Motivation level can be too low to produce good performance, and it can be so high that it interferes with performance. Between these extremes is an optimal range. Within that range, when new material is being learned, a moderate level of motivation is best. When the material has already been learned, a high level of motivation is best.

Attention means that some aspects of a situation are noticed and others are ignored. According to theory, discriminative learning proceeds by two stages. In the first stage the subject learns to attend to the relevant aspects of the situation. In the second he learns which of these aspects are associated with reward and which are not. He learns first which stimulus dimensions are relevant (e.g., color), and then which values on the relevant dimensions are correct (e.g., red). Mentally retarded children differ from normally intelligent children in the speed of learning in the first stage but not in the speed of learning in the second stage. Thus, the main problem of the retarded child apparently is determining which aspects of a situation are relevant and which should be ignored.

Task characteristics. Four task characteristics that influence discriminative learning are stimulus similarity, separation between stimuli, separation between stimulus and response locations, and the nature of the stimuli.

Discriminative learning is harder when the stimuli are extremely similar or extremely dissimilar than when they are in a middle range of similarity. Apparently, both extreme similarity and extreme dissimilarity interfere with dimensional learning, the first stage of discriminative learning.

Discriminative learning is also impaired when the stimuli

are located far apart. The reason is that separation between the stimuli makes comparison harder.

When the subject must look at one location to see a stimulus and must look at another location to indicate his choice, learning is impaired. Separating the locations of the stimuli from the locations of the responses interferes with learning because it makes the irrelevant position cues more salient.

Discriminative learning is easier when there are more relevant dimensions distinguishing the positive and negative stimuli. Thus, discriminative learning with three-dimensional, stereometric objects is easier than it is with flat, planometric objects. The reason for this difference is that the subject is more likely to begin early to attend to one of the relevant dimensions when there are more relevant dimensions to consider.

Procedural variables.   We have discussed the procedural variables of shaping and fading. Shaping is a procedure applied to responses, and fading is applied to stimuli. The purpose of shaping is to get the subject to emit a response that initially he does not emit. It is accomplished by rewarding closer and closer approximations to the desired response. In fading, a stimulus that is not intended to control responses is gradually introduced–faded *in*–while the desired stimulus continues to control the responses, or it is gradually eliminated–faded *out*–while the desired stimulus gradually takes over the controlling function.

Shaping provides a nonverbal technique for "instructing" subjects. However, there may be verbal analogues, such as verbally instructing subjects about small segments of the task, proceeding to larger segments only after the smaller ones are thoroughly understood. Fading provides a technique for discriminative learning without any errors being made. It could be a useful procedure in practical situations in which an error would have harmful consequences.

Suggested Readings

General

Reese, H. W. *The perception of stimulus relations: Discrimination learning and transposition*. New York: Academic Press, 1968.

Siqueland, E. R., & Rieber, M. Discriminative learning. In H. W. Reese & L. P. Lipsitt (Eds.), *Experimental child psychology*. New York: Academic Press, 1970.

Motivation

Brown, J. S. *The motivation of behavior*. New York: McGraw-Hill, 1961.

Longstreth, L. E. Motivation. In H. W. Reese & L. P. Lipsitt (Eds.), *Experimental child psychology*. New York: Academic Press, 1970.

Attention

Eimas, P. D. Attentional processes. In H. W. Reese & L. P. Lipsitt (Eds.), *Experimental child psychology*. New York: Academic Press, 1970.

Shaping and Fading

Risley, T. R., & Baer, D. M. Operant conditioning: "Develop" is a transitive, active verb. In B. Caldwell & H. Ricciuti (Eds.), *Review of child development research*. Vol. III. *Social influence and social action*. New York: Russell Sage Foundation, 1973.

Chapter 4 Discriminative Transfer

Transfer is the effect of previous experience on present performance. In this chapter the previous experience we are concerned with is discriminative learning. In general, discriminative learning will transfer to other discriminative-learning tasks and will then influence performance. The influence may be facilitation of or interference with the new discriminative learning. When transfer is facilitative, it is called *positive transfer*; when it is interfering, it is called *negative transfer*.

Transfer can occur only if there are at least two learning tasks, one providing the previous experience and the other providing the present performance. If the stimuli in the two tasks are identical or very similar, and if the responses associated with the stimuli are incompatible, then transfer is negative. Incompatible responses are ones that cannot occur simultaneously. For example, saying a word aloud is incompatible with saying any other word aloud, because you cannot speak two words simultaneously.

When the stimuli in the two tasks are distinctively different, or when the responses in the two tasks are compatible, transfer is likely to be positive. Compatible responses are ones that can occur simultaneously. For example, saying a word aloud and touching a push button can occur at the same time and are therefore compatible. (However, for young children saying words that contradict the motor response may be difficult. For example, saying "Don't push" may interfere with pushing, saying "No" may interfere with nodding "yes," and saying "Yes" may interfere with shaking the head "no.")

Several types of discriminative transfer have been identified, but there is no one system that incorporates all of them. Some types of transfer are identified on the basis of the experimental procedure used to assess them; others are identified on the basis of the theoretical explanation of the cause of transfer. We will look at four types of transfer in this chapter. The first two, *discrimination learning set* and *transfer along a continuum*, are identified by procedure; the second two, *transposition* and *acquired equivalence and distinctiveness of stimuli*, are identified by theory. The theory associated with acquired equivalence and distinctiveness is *mediation* theory, which is discussed in a separate section later in this chapter.

We will see in this chapter that transfer methodology provides a useful way of finding out what children have *actually* learned compared with what they were *supposed* to learn. The study of transfer therefore has important practical implications.

Discrimination Learning Set

Learning set is the name given the type of transfer that results from training on a series of problems of the same kind. Thus, discrimination learning set, which results from training on a series of discrimination-learning problems, is only one of many types of learning set. We know this kind of transfer has occurred when new discrimative-learning problems are solved in a single trial, because the transfer identified as discrimination learning set is so facilitative that one-trial learning occurs.

Training procedures.   Two types of procedure have been used in studies of discrimination learning set. In the more common procedure the subject is given a series of discrimination problems, each with different stimulus objects and each with a small, fixed number of trials. For example, two objects are presented for four trials. Each new pair of objects is a new discriminative-learning problem. The series of problems is continued—four trials with each new pair of objects—until the subject demonstrates that he has acquired the discrimination learning set by solving each new problem in a single trial.

One-trial learning means that on the first trial of a new problem the subject acquires all the information needed for perfect performance on the remaining trials of the problem. On the first trial the subject must guess which object is correct. If he guesses correctly (a "win"), he continues to choose that object on the remaining trials. If he guesses incorrectly (a "loss"), he shifts to the other object and chooses it on the remaining trials. This "win-stay and lose-shift" strategy has been identified as the source of one-trial learning. Theoretically, the subject learns this strategy over the series of problems.

In the other procedure the subject is given training on each problem until he solves it. Only after the subject is consistently choosing the correct object in a problem is the problem changed by substituting new objects. As in the other procedure, the series of problems is continued until the subject demonstrates one-trial learning in new problems.

Species differences.   In all of the primates—including monkeys, apes, and humans—the final result of learning-set training is one-trial learning. However, below the primates on the evolutionary scale few species have been found that are capable of this high level of performance (see Reese, (1970c). Thus, learning set is an advanced type of performance.

Even among the primates the speed of learning-set acquisition is related to evolutionary status. For example, when the first training procedure (a small fixed number of trials on each problem) is used, young children require training on far fewer problems to acquire the learning set than monkeys do. In one study, preschool children required from 10 to 90 problems, with an average of about 20 (Levinson & Reese, 1967). In contrast, monkeys require several hundred problems (Reese, 1964).

There is some evidence that in monkeys the acquisition of a learning set depends on the total number of trials presented, regardless (within limits) of how the trials are partitioned among the problems (Reese, 1964). However, this relation holds only if there is more than one training problem. That is, prolonged training on one problem will not yield a learning set in monkeys. In contrast, children can acquire a learning set in the process of learning a single problem. Thus, for children the acquisition of a learning set does not depend on the total number of trials presented, since a learning set can be acquired by training children to solve a single problem.

It is important to emphasize that in all of the primates —and in some other mammals—the result of learning-set training is one-trial learning. Thus, even though monkeys, for example, require many more problems to acquire the learning set than young children do, after the learning set has been acquired all of these species are identical in their ability to solve new discriminative-learning problems. The species that are capable of acquiring the learning set therefore do not differ from one another in learning ability *after* the learning set has been acquired. They differ only in how long it takes to *acquire* the learning set and, as we will see later, in why it takes different amounts of training.

Age differences.   Levinson and Reese (1967) examined
learning-set acquisition across the human life span. As already mentioned, preschoolers required an average of about
20 problems to acquire the learning set. Fifth-graders required about 11 problems, college students about 7 problems,
and a large and heterogeneous group of elderly persons required about 120 problems.

Among the elderly there was little if any relation between
speed of acquisition and age, which, in this experiment,
ranged from 61 to 97 years. However, educational and environmental variables did seem to be related to speed of
acquisition in the elderly. A group of retired professionals
required an average of about 13 problems; a group from a
golden age center required about 90 problems; a group from
one old-age home required about 130 problems; and a group
from another old-age home required more than 250 problems.
Levinson and Reese described the first old-age home as
"housed in modern buildings, with large living quarters decorated in different styles, each room occupied by one person"
(Levinson & Reese, 1967, p. 41). The second old-age home was
described as "old, crowded, and somewhat dreary" (p. 43). The
implication is that in old age a lack of educational attainment, activity, and environmental stimulation leads to deterioration more than age alone does.

As in the case of species differences, after the learning set
has been acquired, subjects of all ages are identical in their
ability to solve new discriminative-learning problems. The
age groups differ only in how long it takes to acquire the
learning set and in why it takes different amounts of training.

Error analysis.   The immediate causes of differences in the
speed of learning-set acquisition are found by analyzing the
errors that occur before the learning set is acquired. The
errors can be categorized in various ways. One set of
categories, used by Harlow (1959), includes position preference, position alternation, stimulus preference, stimulus alternation, *differential-cue error*, and *response shift error*.

1. Position preference refers to a tendency to respond to the same position, regardless of which object is in that position.

2. Position alternation refers to a tendency to alternate between the positions, left-right-left-right-etc., regardless of the objects.

3. Stimulus preference is a tendency to choose an object regardless of whether it is correct. However, if it is the correct object that is chosen, the response is not an error. Therefore, stimulus preference is identified by consistent choices of the incorrect object in a problem.

4. Stimulus alternation refers to repetitive choice of first one object and then the other, regardless of position or reward.

5. The differential-cue error is "the frequency of errors on the first trial on which the correct stimulus object changes position (differential-cue trial), relative to errors on trials on which the correct stimulus remains in the same position (multiple-cue trials)" (Reese, 1964, p. 332). The definition of multiple-cue trials means that the correct object stays in the same position across a series of trials. The subject could obtain rewards by choosing the correct object or by fortunately choosing the position that the correct object is in. If he is responding to the object on the multiple-cue trials, then on the differential-cue trial, in which the position of the correct object is changed, the subject will again make a correct response. However, if he is responding to position on the multiple-cue trials, then on the differential-cue trial he will make an error, choosing the same position, which is now occupied by the incorrect object. Even if the subject is not responding solely to position, he should acquire on multiple-cue trials a habit of responding to the position occupied by the correct object. Then, on the differential-cue trial, this position habit will interfere with the tendency to choose the correct object and will sometimes produce an error.

6. The response-shift error, like the differential-cue error, is defined by relative frequencies of errors. The response-shift error is shifting from the correct object to the incorrect object more often than staying with the incorrect object. That

is, it is a greater frequency of errors following a correct response than following an error. It is usually measured on the second trial of a problem. A response-shift error occurs on Trial 2 if more errors occur in a series of problems in which the Trial 1 response was correct than occur in a series of problems in which the Trial 1 response was incorrect.

Error analysis: Monkeys versus children. The major source of error in monkeys is response-shift. For example, Harlow (1950) gave a series of problems to rhesus monkeys, with six trials per problem, and found that the relative frequency of response-shift errors was 57 percent in the second hundred problems. Monkeys also exhibit relatively strong stimulus preference but only early in training. Thus in Harlow's study the relative frequency of the stimulus-preference error was 22 percent in the first hundred problems and only 6 percent in the second hundred. Stimulus preference is also more prevalent in young monkeys than in mature monkeys (Harlow, 1959). The differential-cue error is relatively strong in monkeys and persists longer than stimulus-preference errors. However, stimulus alternation and the position errors are relatively rare in monkeys (Reese, 1964). These data for monkeys are summarized in Table 4.1. The table also summarizes comparable data for young children.

Table 4.1
Relative Importance of Error Types in Learning-Set Acquisition by Monkeys and Children

Error Type	Monkeys	Children
Response-shift	Strong	Strong
Differential-cue	Strong	Strong
Stimulus preference	Moderate	Weak
Stimulus alternation	Weak	Moderate
Position preference	Weak	Moderate
Position alternation	Weak	Moderate

Note: Based on Harlow (1950, 1959), Levinson & Reese (1967), and Reese (1963, 1964).

In both young children and monkeys response-shift is a major source of error, and the differential-cue error is strong. Unlike monkeys, however, young children exhibit negligible stimulus-preference errors and relatively strong stimulus alternation and position preference. Position alternation also seems to be stronger in children than in monkeys but not before the older end of the preschool range.

As we have seen, young children require training on far fewer problems to acquire the learning set than monkeys do. Since the error analyses show that monkeys have more limited *sources* of errors than young children, it follows that the error types must persist longer in monkeys than in children. Because the monkeys have fewer types or sources of errors (Table 4.1) but take longer to learn, the error types must persist longer before being rejected. If the error types are identified as incorrect "strategies," then it could be said that monkeys have a limited number of strategies available which they persist in using for long periods. In contrast, the young child has a relatively large number of strategies available which he abandons when they fail to produce consistent reward.

Error analysis: Age differences. Similar analyses were used by Levinson and Reese (1967) in their study of learning-set acquisition across the human life span. They found that there were more varied strategies in the preschoolers and old persons than in the fifth-graders and college students. Furthermore, the strategies were more persistent in the preschoolers and old persons and were most persistent in the old persons. Among the elderly there were five subjects who were given 450 problems and still never acquired the learning set. One of these subjects exhibited position preference throughout the entire 450 problems; another exhibited position alternation throughout; a third exhibited the differential-cue error throughout (win-stay position, lose-shift position); a fourth exhibited this position strategy through a block of 250 problems; and the fifth shifted erratically between this position strategy and position alternation.

Even among the elderly subjects who eventually acquired the learning set, incorrect strategies sometimes persisted for as many as 200 problems.

The tendency to respond to positions instead of objects was strong in the preschoolers and even stronger in the elderly. It is therefore especially important in training these groups to reduce, insofar as possible, the salience of the position cues and to increase the salience of the object cues. (*Salience* is defined in Chapter 3.) To accomplish these objectives, the stimuli could be placed closer together (Levinson and Reese had an 8-1/2 inch separation between the centers of the objects), and the objects could be made larger or more striking in some way.

Relationship with concept formation.   Learning-set acquisition can be analyzed as a kind of concept formation. According to one theory, the subject learns during the course of training to choose the object that has just been rewarded. That is, on the first trial of a new problem the subject sees which object is rewarded, and on the next trial he chooses that object because it has just been rewarded on the trial before. However, the attribute of being just-rewarded is abstract. It is not like color, shape, or other concrete attributes which are physically present before the choice is made. The reward is physically present in association with the correct object only *after* the choice is made. Even then it is physically present only until the subject removes the reward from the hole. Thereafter, the reward is only conceptually associated with the object.

For example, suppose the experimenter presents a red square and a blue triangle side by side and each covering a small hole in which a piece of candy can be hidden. Suppose, too, that the experimenter has arbitrarily decided that choice of the red square is "correct." He therefore hides the candy under the red square and leaves the hole under the blue triangle empty. If the child picks up the red square, he will see the candy while he is still seeing the red square. At this point the reward is physically associated with the object, and the attribute of being "just-rewarded" is consequently a physical attribute of the object. However, after the subject has eaten the candy, the only physical attributes remaining in the object are the redness and the squareness. The attribute of "just-rewarded" has disappeared into the child's mouth and stomach and in doing so has become an abstract concept.

You can see, then, that after the reward has been consumed, the concept of a just-rewarded object is the same as the concept of a correct object. Consequently, the theory actually says only that the subject learns during the course of training to choose the correct object. This "explanation" is circular and empty unless it is reworded to assert that during the course of training the subject learns the abstract concept of correctness and learns to apply it to objects. Thus, on the next trial the subject will not "know" that the red square is correct until he has looked under it to see if the candy is there, *unless* he has associated the abstract concept of just-rewarded or correctness with this object. Learning-set acquisition, then, involves concept formation.

Practical implications. The interpretation of learning-set acquisition as a kind of concept formation reveals some practical implications that might not be so obvious from other possible interpretations. One implication is that experience with many instances of a concept will lead to learning of that concept, even if there is little learning in the early contacts with the instances. A second implication, however, is that thorough learning in these early contacts will speed up the process of concept formation.

The first implication seems to be correct, in that experience with many instances does in fact speed up concept formation. The second implication does not seem to be borne out, however, because reducing the number of instances and correspondingly increasing the amount of training with each instance does not seem to aid concept formation. Furthermore, it is possible that prolonged training may interfere with concept formation by allowing the subject time to attend to all of the particular details of the instances. As a result the subject may not be able to see the forest for the trees. That is, he may be attending to so many details that he may overlook the conceptual category.

The fact that this second implication seems to be wrong could mean that the interpretation is wrong, and learning-set acquisition is in fact not a kind of concept formation. Or it could mean that the concept-formation interpretation of learning-set acquisition is correct, and that the second implication is not actually contradicted by the concept-formation data mentioned in the last paragraph, because the kind of concept formation in learning-set acquisition is different from the kinds of concept formation studied in *concept-formation* tasks. The latter alternative is more apt to be correct, because in the learning-set situation the subject must learn a new concept. In contrast, in most studies of concept formation the subject does not learn a new concept but either learns a new label for an old concept or learns which old concept the experimenter wishes him to apply (see Chapter 7). Thus, most concept-formation studies deal with concept identification rather than with real concept learning. Since school learning is apt to involve real concept learning, it may be that the implications of the learning-set research are more directly relevant than the implications of the concept identification research.

There are, then, two important implications of learning-set research for the teaching of concepts in classroom situations. They are (1) experience with many instances will lead to learning of the concept, even if there is little learning in the early contacts with the instances. That is, giving a large number and variety of examples will be helpful even if the early examples are not clearly understood by the learners. (2) In addition, thorough learning of a few examples will speed up the process of concept formation. That is, if a few examples are given, and they are thoroughly explained and hence thoroughly understood by the learners, then the concept being taught will be grasped more easily.

The learning-set research illustrates another technique that can be useful in education. The identification of different types of errors in learning-set research has been an aid to understanding how learning sets are acquired. Analogously, error analyses could be applied to workbook exercises, thus providing a way to diagnose patterns of errors that are bothering the class or individuals. Identification of these error patterns could then be used as a basis for modifying the instructional contents or for developing remedial instruction.

Transfer Along a Continuum

Transfer along a continuum is a simple kind of transfer in which the subject is trained on an easy form of a discrimination and is then trained on a difficult form of the same discrimination. As a result of this procedure the difficult form is easier to learn than it would be if the training on the easy form were not given first. For example, Spiker (1959) trained preschoolers on a brightness discrimination which was difficult because the brightnesses were similar to one another. One group was given 48 training trials on this discrimination, and another group was given 24 trials *preceded by* 24 trials on an easy brightness discrimination. The latter group was thus given only half as much training on the difficult discrimination itself. Nevertheless, this group was considerably better on the difficult discrimination than the group that did not receive the easy discrimination first. This same result has been obtained in rats and in adult humans.

The effect has been attributed to attention. In the easy form of the discrimination the subject quickly learns to attend to the relevant dimension, brightness. Thus the first stage of discriminative learning—learning what dimension is relevant (see Chapter 3)—proceeds rapidly, and the second stage—learning which dimensional value is correct—can begin sooner. The attention response would be hard to learn in the difficult form of the discrimination, but it transfers from the easy form and therefore does not need to be learned the hard way. The principle is a simple one which is well-known to educators: begin from the easy and progress to the difficult.

Transposition

Transposition has about the same meaning in psychology as it does in ordinary English: a change in absolute properties without a change in relative properties. Thus if a subject's response appears to be based on the relative property, he is said to have *transposed*. If it appears to have been based on the absolute property, he is said to have made an *absolute response*.

Sample study.   The study of transposition has a long history in psychology. A typical problem is illustrated by a study by Reese (1962a), part of which we described in Chapter 3. In this study, as you may remember, five- and six-year-olds learned to choose the middle-sized stimulus from an array of three stimuli. The stimuli were wooden blocks either similar in size (1.3 to 1 ratio of surface areas) or distinctive in size (2 to 1 ratio). The surface areas were 64, 49, and 38 square inches (1.3 to 1 ratio) or 64, 32, and 16 square inches (2 to 1 ratio).

After a child solved the discrimination problem, he was given a test with three other blocks that had the same degree of similarity to one another as the blocks used in training, but which were different in absolute size from the training blocks (for example, 49, 38, and 29 sq. in., maintaining the 1.3 to 1 ratio; 32, 16, and 8 sq. in., maintaining the 2 to 1 ratio). If a subject chose the middle-sized test stimulus, which had a different absolute size from the middle-sized training stimulus, he would be making a transposition response. If he chose the test stimulus that was most similar in absolute size to the middle-sized training stimulus, he would be making an absolute response.

The subjects were actually given two tests for transposition. In one, the stimuli were relatively close in absolute size to the training stimuli; and in the other, the stimuli were distant in size from the training stimuli. To illustrate these tests suppose that there is a series of six blocks, graduated in size. Training is given on Blocks *1, 2,* and *3* with *2* (the middle-sized one) correct. One test includes Blocks *2, 3,* and *4*.

In this test, choice of Block *3*—the middle-sized block in this set—is a transposition response, and choice of Block *2*— the block correct during training—is an absolute response. The other test includes Blocks *4, 5,* and *6*. Choice of Block *5*—the middle-sized block—is a transposition response, and choice of Block *4*—the one most similar to the middle-sized training stimulus—is an absolute response.

The percentage of transposition responses is shown in Figure 4.1. As you can see, there was more transposition with similar stimuli (1.3 to 1 ratio of areas) than with distinctive stimuli (2 to 1 ratio). That is, there was more transposition on the "close" test (with Stimuli *2, 3,* and *4*) than on the "distant"

Figure 4.1
Percentage transposition in the Reese study as a function of age of subjects, nature of test, and similarity of stimuli. Transposition was generally greater with similar stimuli (solid line) than with distinctive stimuli (broken line).

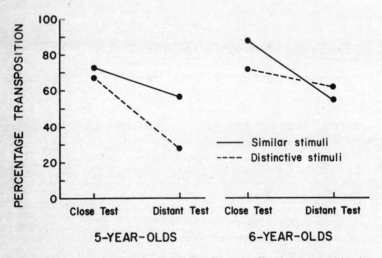

From data reported by Reese, H. W. The distance effect in transposition in the intermediate size problem. *Journal of Comparative and Physiological Psychology*, 1962a, 55, Table 2, p. 529.

test (with Stimuli *4, 5,* and *6*). In addition, there was more transposition in older children than in younger children. The absolute responses are not shown in the figure, but they were influenced in the opposite direction by the same variables. That is, subjects tended to give the absolute response whenever they did not transpose. All of these effects have been confirmed in other studies (see review by Reese, 1968).

Theory. Though there are many different ways to interpret findings such as these (see Reese, 1968), we will discuss only one way here. The finding of more transposition responses, or responses to relations, when the stimuli are more similar can be interpreted to mean that the perception of relational cues is a more important determinant of performance when the absolute cues are highly similar and consequently more likely to be confused with one another. We can interpret the finding of more transposition on the close test than on the distant test, together with the finding that there were more absolute responses on the distant test than on the close test, to mean that the absolute cues were also effective. Finally, we can interpret the finding of more transposition in older children than in younger children to mean that the perception of relational cues is easier for older children than for younger children.

Implications. Some possible practical implications of these interpretations are (1) if children are being taught about relational properties, as in set theory for example, it may be more effective to use materials in which the absolute properties are similar enough to cause confusion, in order to emphasize the relational properties. (2) It is necessary to keep in mind that the intended cues—the relational properties in this case—may not be the effective cues. The absolute properties may also be effective. (3) Because relational learning is easier for older children than for younger children, it is desirable to postpone, as long as is reasonable, learning situations requiring relational learning.

Probably the most important of these implications is the second one, which warns that the intended cues may not be the effective ones. Thus the child may solve a problem not on the basis intended by the teacher (or researcher) but rather on the basis of cues that the teacher considers to be incidental. An example is an informal report that many children in the first and second grades insist that a large "3" signifies a larger quantity than a small "5." The child is responding to the *size* of the numeral, and transposing inappropriately to the *size* of the quantity signified.

The tendency to respond to the size of the numerals means that size is a salient (effective) dimension of numerals. Dimensional salience has been studied extensively in children, and this research shows that size is usually not spontaneously attended to (see Table 3.5, p. 39). Here, however, size is attended to, and its effectiveness can be put to practical use. In mathematics education, for example, the workbook material could be arranged to capitalize on the salience of the size dimension, in conjunction with application of the principles of fading discussed in Chapter 3 and the principles of learning-set acquisition discussed earlier in this chapter. In the first few exercises low numbers could be written small and high numbers written large. The numeral *1* would be smaller than *2, 2* smaller than *3, 3* smaller than *4*, etc. The size difference would be gradually reduced—faded out as a cue—until the numerals were all the same size. At the same time the concept of seriation could be taught by including a variety of physically graded series, each presented in association with the series of numerals. The first graded series would differ naturally in size and would be associated with numerals differing in size. As the exercises continued, the workbook would introduce series graded in other dimensions, ending with dimensions unrelated to size (e.g., density) but still related to the number series.

Mediation Theory

The concept of *mediation* is extremely important in psychology, especially for studies dealing with the more complex kinds of transfer. In this context mediation refers to a process that intervenes between presentation of a stimulus and production of a response.

Figure 4.2 is a diagram of the concept of mediation, in symbolic form. As an illustration of the diagram, let us suppose that the first stimulus in the pictured sequence is a square block. If the subject says "square" when the block is presented, he will hear himself say the word and might also get muscular feedback from the act of saying the word. In the figure, saying the word is symbolized "r_m," and the feedback (hearing or feeling) that is produced by the response is symbolized "s_m." If the subject has already learned to pick up blocks that he labels "square," then the terminal response —picking up the block—will be aroused by the feedback, s_m. Thus the chain is: Block (S) arouses naming (r_m), which produces feedback (s_m), and the feedback arouses picking up (R). The response r_m is called a mediating response because it intervenes or *mediates* between the initial stimulus and the terminal response.

In this example the mediating response and the stimulus it produces are observable. When the mediating response is saying a word aloud, as in the example, the mediating response can be seen by lip-reading, and the stimulus it produces can be heard. Most often, however, the mediating response and stimulus are not observed; they occur mentally,

---

Figure 4.2
The mediation process diagrammed symbolically. The initial stimulus *(S)* arouses (→) a mediating response *(rm)* which produces (↝) a mediating stimulus *(Sm)*, and finally the mediating stimulus *(sm)* arouses (→) the terminal response *(R)*. Lower-case letters are used to represent the mediating response and the stimulus it produces to indicate that these are usually not observed.

$$S \longrightarrow r_m \rightsquigarrow s_m \longrightarrow R$$

and their occurrence must be inferred instead of being actually observed.

Production and control deficiency. The use of mediators requires two kinds of training. First, the mediating response must be conditioned to the initial stimulus. This learning is the association between S and r_m in Figure 4.2. Second, the mediating stimulus must be conditioned to the terminal response. This learning is the association between sm and R in the figure.

Even after the appropriate training is given, however, mediation may fail to occur. This failure in mediation happens when the initial stimulus fails to arouse the potential mediating response. The subject is capable of producing this response, but for some reason he does not produce it. This source of failure in mediation is called a *production deficiency*. Mediation may also fail to occur because the mediating stimulus fails to arouse the terminal response. In this case the subject produces the potential mediator, but for some reason it fails to control the terminal response. This source of failure in mediation is called a *control deficiency*.

In more ordinary language, mediation means that a person's own speech controls his behavior, production deficiency means that he makes no attempt to use speech to control his behavior, and control deficiency means that his speech fails to control his behavior.

Applications. We will discuss one application of mediation theory, including the concepts of production and control deficiency, in the following section. Other applications are discussed in sections of Chapters 6 and 7. One other practical application is in the use of number concepts. Numbers can mediate between arrays containing different numbers of objects, on the one hand, and discriminative responses on the other hand. Suppose that a child must tell which of two arrays contains more objects. The most precise way to get an answer is by counting. Thus counting serves as a mediator betweeen the arrays and the answer.

Acquired Equivalence and Distinctiveness

Definitions. We say that stimuli are *equivalent* if they arouse the same response, and that they are *distinctive* if they do not. In other words, if a particular response is conditioned to one stimulus, other stimuli that spontaneously arouse this response are equivalent to the conditioned stimulus. Stimuli that do not spontaneously arouse this response are distinctive.

Stimuli are intrinsically equivalent if they are highly similar to one another, if they have attributes in common—color, size, shape, etc. Such stimuli will arouse the same responses because they are similar to one another. Conversely, stimuli are intrinsically distinctive if they do not share attributes. They do not arouse the same responses because they are not similar to one another. Two similar shades of gray, for example, are intrinsically equivalent; black and white are intrinsically distinctive.

Stimuli that are not intrinsically equivalent can become equivalent as a result of special training. Equivalence acquired through training is called *acquired equivalence*. The training involves associating the stimuli with a single label. Conversely, two stimuli that are not intrinsically distinctive can acquire distinctiveness through special training, yielding *acquired distinctiveness*. This training involves associating the stimuli with different labels.

Thus, distinctive stimuli that are given the same label acquire equivalence, and similar stimuli that are given different labels acquire distinctiveness. For example, the morel and shaggy-mane are different in many ways, but learning to call both of them "mushroom" yields acquired equivalence and leads to the same responses—picking and eating (which is not always a good idea). Conversely, the agaric and amanita have many features in common, but learning to call the one "mushroom" and the other "toadstool" should yield acquired distinctiveness and aid in distinguishing between them.

Relation to mediation theory. Figure 4.2 shows that the response to the initial stimulus (S) is the mediating response (r_m) and not the terminal response (R). The terminal response is not a response to the initial stimulus but rather a response to the mediating stimulus (s_m). Consequently, all stimuli that arouse a particular mediating response will be followed by the same terminal response. The mediating response aroused by these stimuli will produce its characteristic mediating stimulus, which in turn will arouse its characteristic terminal response. The result is acquired equivalence of the stimuli.

Mediated responding, or acquired equivalence, can be very efficient. Instead of having to learn a new set of responses to each new stimulus, you can simply identify the category to which the new stimulus belongs, and then respond on the basis of the category label. Thus the category label functions as a mediator. While efficient, however, this mode of responding is not always desirable, as in the case of mushrooms. Another obvious example is stereotyping, in which the prejudiced individual responds to a category label that he has assigned to other persons.

There are some cases, however, in which mediated responding can be very useful. For example, if you are told a person's profession—doctor, lawyer, thief, or whatever —when he is introduced to you, this cue can help you to make appropriate conversation. Similarly, being told that one piece of modern furniture is a chair and another is a table can mediate appropriate responses to these objects. As a mediating response, the word "chair" leads to a response of sitting, and the word "table" does not, because one has learned to sit on things labeled "chair" and not to sit on things labeled "table." Note in this example that the word "chair" yields acquired equivalence for one group of objects, and the word "table" yields acquired equivalence for another group of objects. In addition, the different labels yield acquired distinctiveness between these two groups of objects.

In brief, in acquired equivalence the one label for different stimuli mediates the same response, and in acquired distinctiveness the different labels mediate different responses.

The Kendler study. In one kind of procedure used to study acquired equivalence and distinctiveness, labels are learned for stimuli in the first stage of training. New responses are learned for some of these stimuli in the second stage, and the other stimuli are presented in the third stage to test for transfer of the effects of labeling. When the training in the first stage is designed to produce acquired equivalence, the test stimuli in the third stage will arouse the responses learned to the stimuli used in Stage 2. When the Stage 1 training is designed to produce acquired distinctiveness, the test stimuli will not arouse the Stage 2 responses.

Table 4.2 illustrates this procedure as used in a study by Kendler (1972). The stimuli were four meaningless figures. In *Stage 1* the four stimuli were presented and subjects were taught one label (the word "one") for two of them and another label (the word "two") for the other two. In *Stage 2* one stimulus from each of these pairs was used. Subjects were trained to push one button (left) in response to one stimulus and to push another button (right) in response to the other stimulus. In *Stage 3* the Stage 2 training continued, but alternating randomly with the presentations of the two stimuli from Stage 2, the other two stimuli were presented to test for transfer.

The purpose of Kendler's study was to determine experimentally how frequently production deficiency and control

---

Table 4.2
Acquired Equivalence of Stimuli: Transfer-Test Method Used by Kendler (1972)

Stage 1	*Stage 2*	*Stage 3*
Stimulus 1 → "one"	Stimulus 1 → Left Button	Stimulus 1 → Left Button
Stimulus 2 → "one"		Stimulus 2→ ?
Stimulus 3 → "two"	Stimulus 3 → Right Button	Stimulus 3 → Right Button
Stimulus 4 → "two"		Stimulus 4 → ?

deficiency occur. Production deficiency, as noted in the section on mediation theory, is a failure to produce the labels, and control deficiency is a failure of the labels to control the terminal response. By making certain assumptions, Kendler was able to estimate the frequencies of these deficiencies (see Kendler, 1972, for the relevant procedural details and estimation equations).

Figure 4.3 shows the results, with the estimates of production and control deficiency in probability form. You can see

---

Figure 4.3
Estimated probabilities of production deficiency and control deficiency in the Kendler study.

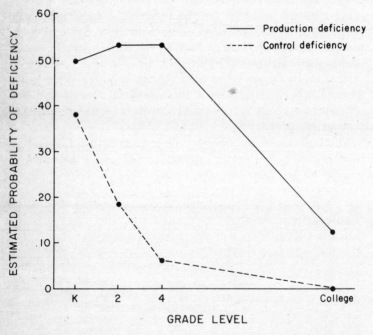

After Kendler, T. S. An ontogeny of mediational deficiency, *Child Development*, 1972, 43, Fig. 5, p. 15. Copyright 1972 by the Society for Research in Child Development, Inc. Used by permission.

---

that production deficiency occurred more frequently than control deficiency, but that there was considerable control deficiency at the youngest age level. In addition, there was some production deficiency even in college students, but no control deficiency. In other words, college students sometimes failed to produce the mediating response, but whenever they did produce it, it controlled the terminal response. In contrast, the young children—especially the kindergarteners—often failed to produce the mediating response, and even when they produced it, it sometimes failed to control the terminal response.

Other studies of mediation in children have yielded similar results. Below the age of about five to seven children generally do not use mediation to control their responses. Children older than this age generally do use mediation (see review by Reese, 1962b). Research has shown that the younger child's problem is usually that he fails to produce the potential mediating response (see Flavell, 1970). In other words, the young child has a problem more often because he makes no attempt to use speech to control his behavior (production deficiency) than because he tries and fails (control deficiency).

An alternative procedure.   In another kind of procedure used in studies of acquired equivalence and distinctiveness the subjects are given two training tasks, as shown in Table 4.3. In the first task, which is the same as the first task in Kendler's design (Table 4.2), the subjects learn different labels for pairs of stimuli. In the second task the subjects learn different motor responses for two of these stimuli. The two stimuli used in the second task can be ones that are labeled differently, as in the Kendler design, or ones that are labeled identically. If they are labeled differently, then they should have acquired distinctiveness, and the pretraining should facilitate second-task learning. Alternatively, if they are labeled identically, then they should have acquired equivalence, and the pretraining should interfere with second-task learning.

Reese (1972), using a design similar to the one shown in

Table 4.3, confirmed the predicted effects. Different labels facilitated discrimination learning, and identical labels interfered. The subjects were from kindergarten through second grade, and there were no marked age differences in the amounts of positive and negative transfer.

Implications. The practical implications are clear. If the same response is supposed to be made to different materials, then the materials should be given a single label. Not only will the label tend to produce transfer from one type to the other types, but also it will interfere with the learning of different responses to the materials. Since the learning of different responses is undersirable in the case under consideration, interference with this learning is desirable. In contrast, in cases where different responses should be made, different labels should be taught. The different labels will not only reduce transfer between the materials but will also facilitate the learning of different responses to the materials.

Specific examples are easy to find. In learning the names of

Table 4.3
Acquired Equivalence and Distinctiveness:
Discriminative-Learning Method

Stage 1	*For Acquired Equivalence*	*Stage 2* *For Acquired Distinctiveness*
Stimulus 1 → Label A	Stimulus 1 → Left Button	Stimulus 1 → Left Button
Stimulus 2 → Label A	Stimulus 2 → Right Button	
Stimulus 3 → Label B		Stimulus 3 → Right Button
Stimulus 4 → Label B		

Note: All subjects receive the same Stage 1 training. Half receive the Stage 2 test for acquired equivalence, and half receive the Stage 2 test for acquired distinctiveness.

---

letters children are asked to ignore the perceptual distinctions between lower-case and upper-case and between print and script. Conversely, they are asked to make distinctions between letter pairs that are perceptually similar, such as *b* and *d*, *b* and *p*, *b* and *q* (representing left-right reversal, up-down reversal, and 180 degree rotation). In mathematics training they must learn that a numeral signifies the same value whether it is written large or small. They are asked to learn that in mathematics equations empty boxes and open spaces are cues for the same kind of response.

The problems seem enormous, unless one considers the work on acquired equivalence and distinctiveness. For example, the distinction between *b* and *d* becomes easier to learn by associating the letters with distinctive motor movements, such as hand on right hip or left hip to mimic the shape of the letter. Or, with a more direct application of acquired distinctiveness, the child might first be taught a simple button-pushing discrimination between *b* and *d*. When the letters are presented simultaneously, the child must push the button under the *b*, for example. This task should present no difficulties. Once the child has learned this discrimination, it should then be easier to teach him the more difficult discrimination requiring hand on right hip for *b* and on left hip for *d*. And having learned this discrimination, it should be easier for him to learn the otherwise difficult discrimination of saying "bee" for one letter and "dee" for the other.

Such complicated procedures may not be needed for ordinary instruction, but they could be useful for remedial work. Furthermore, even for ordinary instruction it should be possible to design better workbooks by keeping in mind and applying the principles of acquired equivalence and distinctiveness, especially if the fading procedure (Chapter 3) is also used. For example, you could begin by associating *b* and *d* with pictured objects, such as a bee and a deer, that are visually distinct but whose names contain the appropriate sounds. Then you could gradually fade out the pictured associates as learning progressed. The learning should progress rapidly because of the acquired distinctiveness, and the acquired distinctiveness will not be needed as a permanent crutch because of the fading procedure.

Summary of Discriminative Transfer

Transfer is the effect of previous experience on present performance. It can facilitate present performance or interfere with it.

Discrimination learning set.   Discrimination learning set is one-trial learning of new discriminative-learning problems following training on a series of discriminative-learning problems with different stimuli. Subjects of different ages or species require different numbers of problems in the series to acquire the learning set, but after the training is complete the age and species differences disappear. That is, once the learning set has been acquired, subjects of any age or species will learn new problems in a single trial.

Subhuman primates have a limited number of incorrect strategies or attempted solutions. In addition, they tend to keep trying an incorrect strategy for a long time before rejecting it. Human subjects have more incorrect strategies available and reject them more readily than monkeys.

Elderly human subjects generally require more training than young children, young children more than older children, and older children more than college students. The age differences are related most strongly to the persistence of incorrect strategies: the elderly subjects are the most persistent, and the college students are the least persistent. In addition, however, the elderly and the young have stronger tendencies to respond to positions instead of objects. Among the elderly there is some evidence that continued activity and stimulation may retard the process of mental deterioration that is often found in old age.

Learning set is like rule learning or concept formation, except that instead of being told the rule or concept, the subject must discover it through experience with many instances.

Transfer along a continuum. Transfer along a continuum means that training on an easy form of a discrimination facilitates subsequent learning of a difficult form of the same discrimination. It is attributed to the transfer of appropriate attentional responses, which are easy to learn in the easy form of the discrimination but would be hard to learn in the difficult form.

Transposition. The transposition task was originally designed to demonstrate that subjects can perceive relational properties of stimuli. It has been found, however, that subjects actually can learn to respond both to relational properties and to absolute properties. The relational properties seem to be more important when the absolute properties are highly similar and therefore likely to be confused with one another. In addition, relational properties are a more important determinant of performance in older children than in younger children. An important practical implication of the research on transposition is that the intended cues, which seem salient to an adult, may not be the effective cues.

Mediation theory. In mediation an initial stimulus arouses a mediating response, which produces a mediating stimulus, and the mediating stimulus in turn arouses the terminal response. The association between the initial stimulus and mediating response is learned. Failure of the initial stimulus to arouse the mediating stimulus, following appropriate training, is a production deficiency. The association between the mediating stimulus and the terminal response is also learned, and failure of the mediating stimulus to arouse the terminal response is a control deficiency.

Acquired equivalence and distinctiveness. Distinctive stimuli that are given the same label acquire equivalence, and similar stimuli that are given different labels acquire distinctiveness. The effects of the labels are attributed to mediation.

Acquired equivalence facilitates new learning when the new learning requires the subject to respond in the same way to different stimuli. Conversely, it interferes when the new learning requires different responses to the stimuli. Acquired distinctiveness has the opposite effects.

When mediation fails to occur, these effects are not obtained. This failure in mediation can happen as the result of either a production deficiency or a control deficiency. Young children exhibit production deficiency more often than control deficiency, but they do exhibit some control deficiency. That is, they often fail to produce an appropriate mediator, but even when they produce an appropriate mediator, it may fail to control further behavior. Even college students sometimes exhibit production deficiency, but they do not exhibit control deficiency. Thus, college students sometimes fail to produce an appropriate mediator, but when one is produced it controls further behavior.

Suggested Readings

General

Jeffrey, W. E. Transfer. In H. W. Reese & L. P. Lipsitt (Eds.), *Experimental child psychology*. New York: Academic Press, 1970.

Learning Set

Reese, H. W. Set. In H. W. Reese & L. P. Lipsitt (Eds.), *Experimental child psychology*. New York: Academic Press, 1970.

Transposition

Reese, H.W. *The perception of stimulus relations: Discrimination learning and transposition*. New York: Academic Press, 1968.

Chapter 5 Verbal Learning

In psychology *verbal learning* does not refer to language development or acquisition of vocabulary. Rather it refers to learning in tasks in which the material presented is verbal or in which the responses required are verbal. Memorizing a list of words or a poem, for example, would be classified as verbal learning. Another example is learning nonsense names for figures, because the names are verbal even though they are not real words.

There has been a tremendous amount of research on verbal learning, perhaps because it seems to be a uniquely human phenomenon, unlike many other kinds of learning. (Actually, verbal learning may *seem* more of a human phenomenon than it really is. Teaching a dog to respond to verbal commands would qualify as verbal learning under our general definition given above.) Most of the research in this area has been done with college students as subjects, but there has also been a large number of studies with children.

For many purposes children are better subjects for studies of verbal learning, partly because the processes that control verbal learning, which are well developed in college students, are still undergoing development in children. In addition, college students often have already learned many of the tricks that aid verbal learning, while children have not. Consequently, the process can usually be studied in children with simpler materials than are required in studies with college students. In addition, children are likely to get more benefit from instructions about the tricks of verbal learning. For these reasons, the research reviewed in this chapter is concerned with verbal learning by children.

Of the many topics of verbal learning, we will discuss only three in this chapter. These three were selected because they have particular relevance to classroom instruction. They also represent three distinctive tasks, and consequently they provide a fairly broad introduction to the study of verbal learning.

The topics and tasks are: (1) clustering in free recall, (2) elaboration in paired-associate learning, and (3) recall of prose. In the free-recall task the subject studies a list of items and is then asked to recall the items in any order. In paired-associate learning the subject studies a list of pairs of items and then must recall the missing item when one member of a pair is presented. In prose learning the subject studies a prose passage and then must repeat the story either in his own words or in the words as given. We will describe each of these tasks more completely later in the chapter. Also, the meanings of *clustering* and *elaboration* will be given in the appropriate sections.

Clustering in Free Recall

Sample study. An excellent example of a study of clustering in free recall by children is a study by Rossi (1964). Because the study illustrates the procedure so well, we have described it in greater detail than the sample studies given in preceding chapters.

Rossi prepared a list of 20 words, including 5 words from each of 4 conceptual categories. The categories were animal, food, clothing, and body part. The words selected are shown in Table 5.1. Because Rossi was going to test children's memory for these words, he wanted to be sure that the words were equally memorable. One characteristic that affects memory for a word is the frequency with which it occurs in print. High-frequency words are easier to remember than low-frequency words. Rossi therefore equated the words for their frequency of occurrence in juvenile literature.

In the presentation of the list of words, the five items of each category were scattered throughout the list. The first time the list was read to the children, the words were in the following order: *milk, head, bear, dress, bread, leg, coat, cake, horse, mouth, hat, sheep, nose, meat, belt, cat, soup, shoe, thumb, pig.* Rossi wanted to see if the children would spontaneously recall the words by categories. Would the children recall all the animals together, then the foods, and so on, or would they recall them in the order of presentation, or in random order, without regard for conceptual category?

The children in the study were 5, 8, and 11 years old. The youngest ones obviously could not read, and therefore the list of words was read to each of the children. (It would be poor experimental procedure to read the words to the youngest group and to require the older groups to read printed words.)

Table 5.1
Categories of Words Used by Rossi (1964)

Animal	Food	Clothing	Body Part
bear	milk	dress	head
horse	bread	coat	leg
sheep	cake	hat	mouth
cat	meat	belt	nose
pig	soup	shoe	thumb

The child was required to repeat each word after the researcher read it to him. After the entire list had been read, the child was asked to say the words he remembered. This procedure—hearing the list of words and then saying the words remembered—was repeated five times, with the words in a different random order each time.

In addition to the age variable, Rossi included another variable of experimental interest. Half of each age group was given the materials discussed so far. The other half was given a modified list of words. In the modified list one word from each category was taken out, and the category label was substituted. The category labels used were *animal, food, clothing*, and *body*. Rossi expected that including the category labels in the list would increase the amount of recall by categories. Recall by categories is called associative clustering, categorical clustering, or simply clustering. In brief, then, Rossi expected to find that including category labels would promote clustering. He also expected clustering to increase with increasing age level.

In fact, Rossi did find that the amount of clustering increased with increasing age. Older children had a stronger tendency to recall the words in category clusters. Surprisingly, however, including the category labels had no effect on the amount of clustering. Rossi suggested that the categories might have been so easy that the subjects did not need the labels, and that with more difficult categories including the labels might increase clustering.

Additional research. The age difference obtained by Rossi has been confirmed by other researchers. In addition, it has been shown that clustering is typical in free recall by adults as well as by older children. Thus, more mature subjects who hear words in a random order tend to recall them in clusters of related words. Since the words are presented in random order, the organization or clustering into related groups must be done by the subject. That is, the mature subject uses some kind of mental activity to organize the words into meaningful units.

There is some controversy as to whether a subject does the

organizing at the time of presentation, during memory storage, or at the time of recall. In other words, he may organize the words as he hears them, storing words from different categories in different memory "locations." Or he may store relations or meanings, and these may organize the words during storage. Finally, he may store the words haphazardly, organizing them at the time of recall by searching his memory systematically for first one category of words, then another, and so on. At present it appears that there is no one method of organization, but that the material sometimes becomes organized during storage and sometimes is stored independently but retrieved systematically.

Related to clustering is the phenomenon of *subjective organization*. Subjective organization occurs in the recall of lists that consist of semantically unrelated words. The kind of list used by Rossi in his study is objectively organized. The organization is supplied by the experimenter when he decides what conceptual categories to include. The subject learning such a list can use this same organization as a basis for clustering. In unorganized lists—lists of words all from different conceptual categories—the subject has no objective basis for clustering. If clustering occurs in such lists, it is because the subject invents his own subjective organization which he imposes on the list as a basis for the clustering. Research has shown that subjective organization occurs both in children and in adults. However, it is much more frequent and extensive in adults.

Researchers have found that clustering aids free recall. In other words, the tendency to recall in clusters is effective as a memory aid. Thus, to facilitate memorization materials should be organized on the basis of interrelations of meanings. This organizing should be especially helpful for younger children, who do not have a strong tendency to impose organization on unorganized material, and who therefore are likely to remember it in an unorganized way. Older children and adults, in contrast, are likely to impose organization on unorganized material, and therefore do not have as great a need to have the material presented in an organized way.

Memory span.   A peculiarity of memory over short times is that there is a limit to the number of units that can be retained. If the units are items that are completely unrelated to one another, then about seven items can be retained in short-term memory. However, if the units are sets of items, each set including several interrelated items, then about seven *sets* can be retained. For example, it is easier to remember a seven-digit number than to remember seven one-digit numbers. The reason is that the seven-digit number is either one unit or, more likely, is broken into a three-digit unit and a four-digit unit. In contrast, the seven one-digit numbers are seven units. It follows that clustering aids retention by separating the items into sets, thus allowing memory to deal with units larger than individual items. The practical implication is that separating material into integrated segments should make the material easier to hold in short-term memory. In the classroom this technique is particularly useful when the teacher is covering a complex topic that requires holding many details in memory simultaneously. If the details are presented in segments that include interrelated material, the material is more likely to be remembered.

Elaboration in Paired-Associate Learning

The paired-associate task.   In paired-associate learning the subject is presented a series of pairs of items. His task is to learn the pairs so that when one member of a pair is presented, he will be able to recall or recognize the other member. The item that is presented as a cue for recall is called the *stimulus item*, and the item that is to be recalled is called the *response item*. Thus, the paired-associate task consists of presenting stimulus-response pairs and requiring the subject to learn the associations so that when the stimulus item is presented, he can recall the appropriate response item. It is customary to give the stimulus item first and then the response item, if they are presented sequentially, or to give the stimulus item to the left of the response item, if they are presented simultaneously. For example, in the pair *dog-gate*, *dog* is the stimulus item to which the subject is supposed to respond *gate*.

Note that the pairing of *dog* and *gate* is not especially meaningful. You may wonder why subjects would be asked to learn such pairs which are of no practical importance. The reason for this procedure is that psychologists who study paired-associate learning are not interested in teaching the child any useful information. Rather, they are interested in the learning *process*. In order to be able to study this process, they deliberately avoid teaching subjects meaningful relations. One reason is that words that are meaningfully related to each other are very likely to have been learned as pairs outside the experimental laboratory. Thus, with such pairs as *hot-dog* or *chair-table* the subject may have little or nothing to learn in the research task. To avoid this problem, the researcher tries to pair items that are not meaningfully related, that do not make much sense. Consequently, these pairs must be learned in the laboratory situation, and the way the subject learns them can be studied. It is this learning process that interests the researcher. Furthermore, if subjects learn meaningful pairings in the same way they learn meaningless pairings, what the researcher discovers about the process of learning meaningless pairs has important practical application.

Of course, you probably realize that paired-associate learning also occurs in the "real" world. For example, a foreign-language vocabulary is learned by the paired-associate method. The English words are paired with their foreign-language equivalents, and the student learns the pairs so that when one member is presented, he can recall the other member. Actually, from the perspective of the learner, no pairing is meaningful before it is learned. That is, even in a pair that is meaningful in the real world, the relationship is meaningless until it has been learned. Therefore, we should be able to generalize the research findings with meaningless pairings to real-life situations.

The paired-associate method can be used as a tool for studying processes other than paired-associate learning itself. For example, it has been used to investigate components of the reading process. It has also been used to investigate the effect of *elaboration*.

Elaboration.   In a paired-associate task elaboration means that material is added to the stimulus-response pair. For example, instead of presenting *dog-gate* the researcher might elaborate the pair into a sentence: "The dog is closing the gate." Certain kinds of elaboration have been found to be extremely effective aids to memory. One kind is elaborating the pair into a sentence or phrase describing an interaction or a relation between the stimulus and response items. The relation described must be more than a conjunction in order to be effective. For example, elaborating "dog-gate" into "dog and gate" is not effective. The conjunctive relation, expressed by "and," does not make the pairing more memorable. However, relations expressed by prepositions and verbs are highly effective. For example, "the dog on the gate" and "the dog is closing the gate" are much easier to remember than "dog-gate" or "dog and gate."

Verbal elaborations may be easy to remember because they impose an organization or structure on the otherwise unorganized and unstructured pair. In other words, verbal elaboration may be effective because it changes a meaningless pairing of words into a meaningful pairing. The underlying principle may be the same as in clustering in free recall.

Another effective kind of elaboration is pictorial. The pair *dog-gate*, for example, might be pictorially elaborated by showing the dog sitting on the gate, or by instructing the subject to imagine this scene. (Incidentally, it has been found that for young children instructions with demonstrations of interactions between the stimulus and response objects are effective, but instructions without demonstrations are not. This finding is consistent with the point about small-step instructions in Chapter 3.) The effect on performance is similar whether the researcher presents the pictorial elaboration or the subject imagines it. However, imagining or being shown the dog and gate side by side is not effective. Apparently, placing the separate images or pictures side by side is analogous to verbally elaborating a conjunctive relation.

Pictorial elaboration is effective when it depicts an action, the result of an action, or a locational relation. These are the direct pictorial analogues of the kinds of verbal elaboration that have been found to be effective. It is therefore possible that pictorial elaboration is effective not because the subject imagines a relation between the stimulus and response items, but because at the same time he verbalizes a description of the interaction pictured. That is, pictorial elaboration may be effective because it prompts verbal elaboration. Alternatively, verbal elaboration may be effective because it prompts pictorial elaboration. However, we will see later that both these possibilities are probably wrong. Instead, it seems likely that the verbal and visual systems are independent, and that each kind of elaboration is effective independent of the other. Before going further into these matters, let us consider the following sample study.

Sample study. Reese and Parkington (1973, Experiment II) studied the effect of pictorial elaboration in nursery-school children. The items presented were line drawings of animals and everyday objects. One group—the control group—saw the stimulus and response pictures side by side. An example appears in the top half of Figure 5.1. Another group—the experimental group—saw a picture representing the stimulus and response items interacting with each other. An example of this type of picture is shown in the bottom half of Figure 5.1. Table 5.2 lists all the items used. The capitalized words name the stimulus and response items, and the other words indicate the pictorial elaboration.

The subjects were shown the list of pairs, one pair at a time. The control group saw only the side-by-side pictures, without elaborations. The experimental group saw the pictorial elaborations. After all the pairs had been shown, the stimulus items—the animals—were shown one at a time, and the subject was required to remember the associated response

Figure 5.1
Examples of the materials used by Reese and Parkington (1973). The upper panel shows a pair as presented to the control group. The lower panel shows the same pair as presented to the experimental group.

items—the everyday objects. This procedure was repeated, with a different random order of the pairs in each presentation, until the subject demonstrated that he had learned all the pairs. The learning criterion was two runs through the list with no errors. One week later, with no intervening training on the list, the stimulus items were presented again to test long-term memory of the pairings.

The results are shown in Figure 5.2. It was found that pictorial elaboration reduced the number of runs through the list required to learn the pairings. Thus, elaboration made the associations easier to learn for the children, who were four- and five-year-olds. Furthermore, although the older children learned faster, elaboration was effective for both age groups. In addition, elaboration seemed to aid long-term memory, in that there were more correct responses in the one-week test when the pairings were elaborated in original learning. However, the effect of elaboration on long-term memory was unreliable. The best conclusion is that although elaboration facilitated learning, it did not facilitate long-term memory.

Additional research.   Research with other subjects, including children, adults, and old persons, has confirmed the finding that pictorial elaboration facilitates learning. Furthermore, like the Reese and Parkington study, this research

---

Table 5.2
Pairings and Elaborations Used by Reese and
Parkington (1973)

Pairs

DOG on all fours with SCISSORS on nose
HORSE on three legs holding BOOK with forehoof
PIG on all fours playing GUITAR
GIRAFFE on all fours with CLOCK on tail
MOUSE crouching on hind legs holding BANANA
RABBIT on hind legs kicking BALL

Figure 5.2

Learning speed in the Reese and Parkington (1973, Exp. II) study as a function of elaboration and age level. The measure of learning speed is the number of runs through the list required to reach the learning criterion; the lower the score, the faster the learning. The group that saw the elaborated pictures (solid line) learned faster than the group that saw the pictures side by side and unelaborated (broken line).

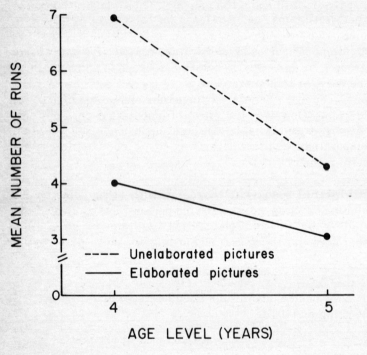

Previously unreported data.

has also yielded inconclusive evidence about the effect of elaboration on long-term memory. In some studies it seems to facilitate long-term memory, in other studies it seems to interfere with long-term memory, and in still other studies it seems to have no effect.

In a study with adult subjects Forbes and Reese (1974) found that pictorial elaboration facilitated learning, as it does in children. In addition, one-week retention was better in subjects who had originally seen the elaborated materials than in subjects who had originally seen the unelaborated, control materials. However, in this study training was not continued until the subjects had learned all the pairs. Instead, the subjects were shown the list twice for study, one pair at a time, and then were immediately given a test to determine how much was learned. As already noted, more was learned in the elaboration condition than in the control condition. Thus, in the one-week retention test the elaboration group performed better than the control group either because elaboration aided memory or because more was originally learned. The control group might have worse memory or less material to be remembered.

To provide a measure of the amount remembered independent of the amount originally learned, Forbes and Reese analyzed the amount *lost*. This measure is the difference between performance on the immediate test and performance on the one-week retention test. It was found that in general the elaboration group lost as much as the control group. Thus, the apparent effect of elaboration on long-term memory was actually an effect on original learning, and long-term memory was not facilitated by elaboration. However, elaboration did not *interfere* with long-term memory; it simply had no effect on long-term memory. Therefore, elaboration resulted in a gain in efficiency of learning, with no loss in memory.

Independence of elaboration types. We mentioned earlier that verbal and pictorial elaboration are independent processes. Two lines of evidence support this contention. The first is provided by studies in which pictorial and verbal elaboration are directly compared. Some of this research has shown that young preschoolers benefit more from verbal elaboration than from pictorial elaboration, while older children benefit equally from the two kinds of elaboration. Figure 5.3 shows the data from one of the relevant studies

Figure 5.3

Effect of age level on the amount of facilitation from elaboration in paired-associate learning (Reese, 1965). Elaboration was pictorial, verbal, or a combination of pictorial and verbal. The data points are corrected for performance in a control no-elaboration condition. Hence, the higher the score, the greater the facilitation. (The measure of facilitation is a ratio: the mean trials-to-learn for the control condition minus the mean for an elaboration condition, divided by the mean for the control condition.)

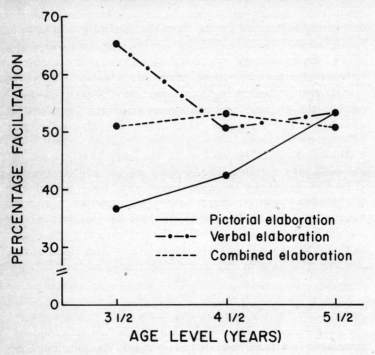

Previously unreported data.

(Reese, 1965). As you can see in the figure, the pictorial elaboration condition produced less facilitation than the two verbal elaboration conditions at the youngest age levels and produced equal facilitation at the oldest age level.

The reduced effectiveness of pictorial elaboration in young children might be attributed to inefficiency in transforming pictorial elaboration into verbal elaboration. That is, the young child might not spontaneously verbalize descriptions of the pictorial elaborations. However, other causes are more plausible (see Reese, 1970b), especially because other research in which pictorial and verbal elaboration were compared has demonstrated equal effectiveness even in young children. For example, Reese (1970a) obtained the data illustrated in Figure 5.4. In this study the trend of the data showed that pictorial elaboration was *more* effective than verbal elaboration at the younger age level. (However, the difference between the conditions was not statistically significant, and therefore the statistically justified conclusion is that the two kinds of elaboration were equally effective.) It appears that when pictorial elaboration is less effective than verbal elaboration, it is because the child is inattentive to the pictorial materials that are presented and not because of any inherent inferiority of pictorial elaboration (see Reese, 1970b).

Further evidence of independence. Studies in which the verbal elaboration condition was not included provide additional evidence that the two kinds of elaboration are independently effective. In these studies pictorial elaboration was compared with a control, no-elaboration condition (pictures side by side) for subjects who were not verbally proficient. The subjects were young deaf children and young preschool children with normal hearing. The results of the studies demonstrate that pictorial elaboration is effective in both kinds of subjects.

Figure 5.5 shows the results of one of these studies, with normal-hearing preschoolers (Reese, unpublished study). The subjects ranged in age from 2.25 years to 6.25 years. The figure shows that even at the youngest age level—the youngest studied thus far—pictorial elaboration facilitated performance. And, as you can see, the curve for the elaboration condition steadily increases with increasing age level. Therefore, the absolute effectiveness of elaboration increased

Figure 5.4
Effect of age level on the amount of facilitation from elaboration in paired-associate learning (Reese, 1970a). Elaboration was pictorial or verbal. The higher the score, the greater the facilitation. (The measure of facilitation is the same as in Figure 5.3).

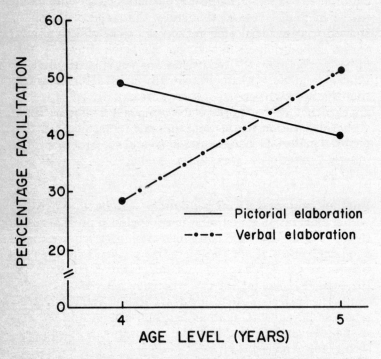

Data points computed from means in Reese, H. W. Imagery in children's paired-associate learning. *Journal of Experimental Child Psychology*, 1970a, 9, Table 2, p. 177.

with increasing age level. However, learning also improved in the control condition, with unelaborated pictures, and therefore the relative effectiveness of elaboration increased very little across the age-span studied.

Figure 5.5
Percentage correct responses as a function of age level with
elaborated pictures and unelaborated pictures.

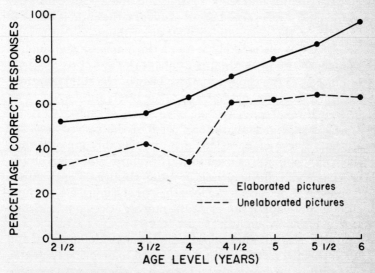

Reese, previously unpublished data.

The youngest children in the study, around 2½ years old,
were at an age level characterized by a lack of verbal profi-
ciency. Consequently they almost certainly did not verbalize
descriptions of the elaborated pictures. We can conclude,
then, that although pictorial elaboration may be less effective than verbal elaboration at young ages, pictorial elaboration is still effective even when the children are so young that
its effects cannot be attributed to spontaneous verbal elaboration by the children.

Additional evidence of independence.   There is another
reason for doubting that spontaneous verbal elaboration can
account for the effect of pictorial elaboration at young age
levels. Specifically, the young child's descriptions of pictures
are likely to be the names of the elements joined by the

conjunction "and." Such conjunctive elaborations are known to provide no facilitation, as we noted earlier. This evidence on children's descriptions comes from two sources. First, one of the items in the Stanford-Binet IQ test consists of showing a fairly complicated scene to the child and asking him what he sees. Below the age of about six years, the child is likely to enumerate the elements without describing their interrelations. That is, he is likely to name the elements and connect them with "and." Beginning at about the age of six, description becomes the usual response. That is, the child mentions not only the elements but also their interrelations.

Second, the same trends have been obtained with the simple pictorial elaborations used in the paired-associate studies. These elaborations are considerably simpler than the complex pictures used in the Stanford-Binet, but enumeration is still characteristic in young children. For example, if shown the picture in the lower panel of Figure 5.1, a young child is more apt to say "a giraffe and a clock" than "a giraffe with a clock on his tail."

In the relevant study children were shown elaborated and unelaborated pictures and were asked to describe each one. The children were divided into two age groups, with average ages of 3.8 years and 5.1 years. Figure 5.6 shows the results. You can see that the differences between the two age groups are small and negligible. For unelaborated pictures both groups used enumeration almost all the time. Enumeration is appropriate for these pictures, because no relations are shown. The crucial data are for elaborated pictures: both age groups used enumeration almost as often as description. Thus, both used inappropriate enumeration for the elaborated pictures almost as often as they used appropriate description.

We can conclude from this that even if the preschooler verbalizes a description of a pictorial elaboration, his description is as likely as not to include only conjunctive relations, which do not facilitate paired-associate learning.

Practical implications. One practical implication of the research on elaboration is that sets of essentially unrelated

Figure 5.6

Children's descriptions of elaborated and unelaborated pictures. The left side shows the percentage of elaborated and unelaborated pictures that were described *without* mention of interrelations among the elements (*enumeration*). The right side shows the percentage described *with* mention of interrelations (*description*).

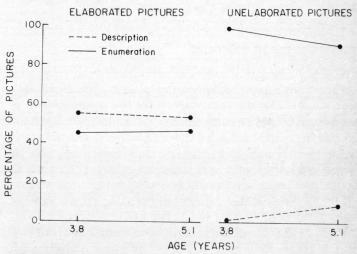

Reese, 1975, previously unpublished data.

material can become interrelated through pictorial or verbal elaboration. The material thus elaborated also becomes easier to remember, at least for short times. Many teachers know about the effectiveness of verbal elaboration. For example, they may teach children to spell "arithmetic" by elaborating the individual letters into a sentence: "A rat in Tom's house might eat Tom's ice cream." An ingenious arrangement of pictures can have the same effect.

In the earlier discussion of the practical implications of clustering in free recall, we noted that separating material into interrelated segments should aid discussion of a complex topic. The research on elaboration suggests that these segments can be made even more memorable through verbal or pictorial elaboration. In addition, it suggests that material that does not fit into integrated segments can be integrated into arbitrary segments by verbal or pictorial elaboration.

The technique should be useful for all elementary school pupils, because research (Rohwer, 1973) has shown that it is effective for lower-class disadvantaged children as well as for middle-class children. Indeed, elaboration sometimes eliminates social-class differences in speed of learning.

Thematic Recall of Prose

It is well known that verbatim recall of prose or poetry —every word correct and correctly placed—is considerably harder than thematic recall—recall of the theme or plot. A single reading may be sufficient to get the plot and important details of a passage, provided they can be reconstructed in the reader's own words. Nevertheless, more repetitions may be needed to get the thematic details in the correct order and to get the less important details.

It has been found that pictures illustrating a prose passage can sometimes aid recall of the themes (e.g., Paivio, 1971; Rohwer, 1973). though there have been studies in which this did not occur. Following is a description of a study with nursery-school children (H. W. Reese, "Imagery and Recall of Connected Discourse," unpublished study, 1970). The use of illustrations in this study apparently did not help the children recall the story they heard.

Sample study. In the study nursery-school children were read the story which is quoted below. For half the children the story was illustrated by a series of pictures. The pictures were drawn and colored by a student artist and were like the pictures in children's storybooks. The pictures were presented at the points indicated in the following quotation. The other children heard the story but were shown only the first and last pictures. That is, for the unillustrated story, the first picture was shown throughout the story until the end, when the last picture was shown. One child at a time was taken to the testing room for the story. As soon as the story was finished, the child was asked to retell it. The child's version was tape-recorded and later transcribed and scored.

The story. This is a story about a cat. The cat's name is Kitty. (*Picture of Kitty presented.*) Kitty lived with his brother and sister. They lived in a big tin can. (*Picture of Kitty removed; picture presented showing Kitty, brother, and sister sitting in front of a tin-can house*.) One night Kitty's brother said, "Let's play hide-and-seek; Kitty can try to find us. There's enough light because the moon is full." Kitty sat in front of the tin-can house and closed his eyes while his brother and sister went to hide. (*Picture of Kitty with eyes closed, sitting in front of tin-can house; brother and sister running to hide; sky black, with stars and full moon.*) Kitty counted to 10, then opened his eyes and started looking for his brother and sister. He said to himself, "Now, where would I hide? I know! I would hide in the hollow tree on the hill." So he went to look in the hollow tree. (*Picture of Kitty walking toward hollow tree on hill.*) Kitty was looking in the hollow tree. Suddenly, an owl sitting on a limb said, "Hoo!" (*Picture of Kitty looking into hollow tree; owl on limb saying "HOO.*") Kitty was so frightened that his fur stood on end, his tail fluffed up, and he ran up the hill away from the tree with the owl in it. (*Picture of Kitty with fur on end, tail fluffed up, running up hill away from hollow tree with owl on limb.*) Kitty ran so fast that he didn't know where he was. He looked around and saw a light. He said to himself, "I'll go where the light is; it won't be scary there." (*Picture of Kitty running down hill toward a lighted horizon.*) He went down the hill toward the light. The light came from a drive-in movie that was showing a Popeye cartoon. (*Picture of Kitty standing in parking lot of a drive-in movie, with refreshment stand, cars, Popeye cartoon on screen.*) There were lots of cars, and Kitty finally felt safe again. Kitty was tired from running up and down the hill. He sat down by the refreshment stand and went to sleep. (*Picture of Kitty yawning and sitting beside refreshment stand.*) Next morning, Kitty woke up and looked around. All the cars were gone. The bright sun hurt Kitty's eyes. (*Picture of Kitty in deserted lot of drive-in movie, rubbing eyes; bright sun in sky; refreshment stand and empty screen in background.*) Kitty found a pair of sunglasses and put them on. (*Same picture, except now Kitty is wearing sunglasses.*) The sun didn't hurt his eyes any more. Kitty said to himself, "Now which way do I go to get home? I'll climb up on the top of the screen to see what I can see." (*Picture of Kitty climbing to top of movie screen.*) From the top of the screen, he saw the hill, the hollow tree, and his tin-can home. The owl was not in the tree any more. (*Picture of hill, hollow tree, tin-can house; Kitty on top of screen in background.*) He ran home, and when he got there he gave the sunglasses to his sister. (*Picture of the three cats sitting; sister-cat wearing sunglasses.*) He told her and his brother all about what he had seen. Then they all sat down at the table to eat breakfast. They each had a glass of milk to drink and an apple to eat. (*Picture of the three cats sitting at a table; glass of milk and apple in front of each cat.*) Then they all went to bed and went to sleep, because cats like to take a nap after eating. (*Picture of three beds, each with a cat lying in it asleep.*)

Examples of children's versions.   Following are four examples of the children's versions of the story.

Subject AL (male, age 4.1 years): "Kitty, Kitty ran away to his brothers and sisters. . . . behind a tree and the owl scared him . . . He ran, ran fast after the light and no cars . . . . Went to sleep and found sunglasses to his sister and went to sleep . . . . ate milk and . . . . apples." (Each dot represents 5 seconds of silence.)

Subject JR (female, age 4.2 years): "The Kitty saw the owl on the tree and the boy and the girl were hiding and they went to bed. Silly cats ate at the table."

Subject MB (male, age 3.9 years): "They went hide and go seek and his brother and sister went away and hide by the...the tree and his fur stood up, and then he got up and he saw the Popeye screen and went to sleep by the treat stand. Then, when he woke up, the sun was too hot so he found a pair of glasses and put them on and went home and gave them to his sister. Then, ate lunch, milk and apple."

Subject BJ (female, age 4.0 years): "(Garble for 10 seconds.) I got kitty cat....I got kite, home tree...and I got it up in the air. I can get down. I got dress and (garble for 3 seconds). I got new shoes...token ring..I got my hand and feets (garble for 2 seconds), chair in my room. Got sick and my mommy (garble for 25 seconds). I make my bed (garble for 10 seconds)."

The first two of these subjects had the story without the

illustrations, and the last two had the story with the illustrations. The stories retold by the first two subjects are clearly not as good as the story retold by the third subject, as might be expected. The story told by the fourth subject is completely unrelated to the story about Kitty. Perhaps this subject did not understand the instructions and thought that she was supposed to make up a new story. However, the instructions ("Now tell me the story you just heard. Tell me as much as you remember.") were clear to most children (and to the experimenter).

Results of the sample study.   In spite of the apparent superiority of one of the subjects who saw the illustrations, in the group as a whole the stories retold by 16 subjects who saw the illustrations were no better than those of 14 subjects who did not see the illustrations. Thus the illustrations did not aid thematic recall.

The children were also asked a series of questions about the story, after they had told their version. For example, they were asked, "Did Kitty have two brothers or one brother and a sister?" The scores of the four sample subjects on the questions were: *Subject AL*: 83 percent correct; *Subject JR*: 42 percent; *Subject MB*: 100 percent; and *Subject BJ*: 46 percent. It appears that the subjects who had seen the pictures (MB and BJ) were somewhat better than the ones who had not seen the pictures. However, the group differences were negligible. Note that Subject BJ, who gave the irrelevant story, scored 46 percent correct on the questions. It appears that this subject's poor performance in retelling the story was not a result of misunderstanding the instructions. Rather, it seems that she simply did not remember much of the story.

The study also showed no effect of sex of subject. In fact, the only positive result of the study was a large age difference: five-year-olds remembered considerably more than four-year-olds.

Additional research.   There is evidence that pictures do not aid recall of stories even in college students when the stories are highly concrete and coherent. That is, if the story deals with physical happenings and observable characteristics of the actors, and if the story hangs together tightly, then adult subjects may not need illustrations. One possible explanation of this effect is that adults can easily imagine their own pictures to illustrate the story. In contrast, if the story is not so concrete or coherent, then illustrations aid recall by college students.

The story about Kitty is mixed. There are concrete events, but there are also some abstractions. For example, Kitty's being frightened is an abstraction; but Kitty's fur standing on end is concrete. The story is also not particularly coherent. The plot or theme is simple: Kitty was playing one night, was frightened by an owl, ran and got lost, slept until daylight permitted him to get his bearings, and then went safely home. The full moon, the game of hide-and-seek, the owl, and some other details are relevant to the theme. However, the story contains many details that are actually irrelevant to this theme: The tin-can house, the Popeye cartoon, the breakfast of milk and apples, the napping after breakfast, and some other details. These irrelevant details could have been omitted without affecting the theme. They are not coherent details. The story, in other words, was not well suited to demonstrating the effects of illustrations.

As researchers often say, the problem remains unsolved and more research is needed. Although the suggestion here is that the variation in picture effectiveness is related to the nature of the story, another possibility is that it is related to individual differences, in reading ability for example (e.g., Levin, 1973).

Verbatim Recall of Prose

We will cover here two aspects of the research on verbatim recall. One is *distributed* versus *massed practice*, and the other is *whole* versus *part learning*.

Distributed versus massed practice. If a fixed amount of time is available for learning, is it better to spend the time all at once (massed practice) or is it better to spend it in small segments separated by other activities (distributed practice)? Research has shown that distributed practice is almost always better than massed practice. Distributed practice is particularly beneficial when there is a great amount of material to be learned.

It appears that massed practice is inefficient partly because the prolonged attention it requires is fatiguing and partly because motivation tends to decrease as the learning session gets longer. Nevertheless, if the distributed practice sessions are too far apart, the benefit of distributed practice may disappear. With very long intervals the learner is likely to forget what he has learned in the preceding session before he begins the next session.

Distribution of practice may also be inefficient when the task requires an extensive warm-up period. That is, if the task requires that the learner be in a particular state of mind, have a particular amount of tension, and so on, then in distributed practice he must spend a relatively large part of each session getting ready to do the task. The consequent reduction in the amount of time available for actually doing the task may be great enough to remove the benefit of distributed practice.

In educational contexts an example of distributed practice would be learning course material, such as equations, throughout the term. Massed practice would be cramming all night on the eve of an examination. The research implies that cramming is not as efficient. If the same total amount of time is spent studying, more will be learned if the study time is distributed than if it is massed.

Whole versus part learning. In whole versus part learning, the question is whether it is better to learn a long poem, for example, from beginning to end or to break it into shorter segments—lines or stanzas—and learn each of these parts separately. The answer is not simple, because the research has sometimes shown the whole method to be superior and sometimes shown the part method to be superior. Nevertheless, the whole method has been found superior more often than the part method. In addition, even when the part method is initially superior, practice with the methods results in superiority of the whole method. However, the topics already covered in this chapter imply that the part method should be superior, provided that the parts, once learned, can be combined in the proper sequence.

After reviewing the relevant research, Hovland (1951) recommended the part method. He suggested, however, that the parts should be as large as can be handled by the learner: "The best advice seems to be to learn by using the largest units that are meaningful and within the individual's capacity. The older the individual, the higher his intelligence, the more practice he has had, the greater is the size of the unit he is able to handle" (p. 642). Thus, the recommendation is to use a part method in which the parts are "wholistic," in the sense of being meaningfully organized.

Summary of Verbal Learning

Verbal learning refers to learning in tasks in which the material presented is verbal or in which the responses required are verbal. It is therefore not limited to language development. The chapter deals with three representative topics and tasks used to study verbal learning.

Clustering in free recall. In the free-recall task the subject studies a list of items and then must recall as many of those as he can remember. He is not required to recall the items in the same sequence as originally presented, hence the recall is "free."

Clustering means that even though the items were originally presented in a haphazard, random sequence, they are recalled in related sets or clusters. Clustering therefore reflects an activity by the subject: he imposes a meaningful order or organization on material that was not presented in a meaningful order.

The amount of clustering increases with age. Even when category labels—names of conceptual classes—are included in the list, young children exhibit less clustering than older children and adults.

Clustering aids free recall, apparently because the organized sets or clusters of words are remembered as units. If clustering did not occur, the subject would have to remember each item as a unit. The short-term memory capacity is around seven units, whether the units are individual items or organized sets of items.

Elaboration in paired-associate learning. In the paired-associate task the subject studies a list of pairs of items, and later when one member of a pair is presented, he is asked to recall the missing member of the pair. The items presented as cues for recall are called stimulus items; the items that are to be recalled are called response items. Elaboration means that material is added to a stimulus-response pair.

Elaborating a pair into a sentence or phrase describing an interaction or a relation between the members of the pair makes the pair easier to learn. However, conjunctive elaboration—joining the items by the word "and"—does not aid learning. The effective kinds of verbal elaboration may be effective because they change a meaningless pairing of words into a meaningful pairing.

Elaboration can be pictorial or imaginal as well as verbal. Pictorial or imaginal elaboration is usually as effective as verbal elaboration, though it, too, is effective only if it represents an interaction or a relation between the members of the pair.

Pictorial elaboration is effective even for children as young as 2½ years old, the youngest age level studied so far. However, it has sometimes been found to be less effective than verbal elaboration at young age levels. Although this finding might suggest that the effect of pictorial elaboration results from spontaneous verbal elaboration (verbal description of the picture), other evidence strongly implies that the two kinds of elaboration are independently effective.

The evidence regarding the effect of elaboration on long-term memory is inconclusive. There is sometimes facilitation, sometimes interference, and sometimes no effect.

Thematic recall of prose. After reading or hearing a prose passage, a subject may be asked to recall it word-for-word (verbatim recall) or he may be asked to recall the plot and salient details (thematic recall). Thematic recall is considerably easier than verbatim recall.

Presenting pictures to illustrate the details of the passage can aid thematic recall. However, pictures do not aid recall when the passage is highly concrete and coherent. The reason for this effect seems to be that subjects spontaneously generate their own images to illustrate such passages.

Verbatim recall of prose. Two topics related to verbatim recall are distributed versus massed practice and whole versus part learning. Distributing the practice into short sessions is generally better than massing the practice into one long session. However, the time between the short sessions must not be so great that a lot of forgetting occurs, and the task must not require so much warm-up time that the short session is largely wasted in warming up to the task.

Part learning is generally superior to whole learning, provided the parts are the largest units that are meaningful and within the individual's capacity.

Suggested Readings

General

Goulet, L. R. Verbal learning in children: Implications for developmental research. *Psychological Bulletin*, 1968, *69*, 359-376.

Kausler, D. H. *Psychology of verbal learning and memory*. New York: Academic Press, 1974.

Keppel, G. Verbal learning in children. *Psychological Bulletin*, 1964, *61*, 63-80.

Palermo, D. S. Verbal learning and memory. In H. W. Reese & L. P. Lipsitt (Eds.), *Experimental child psychology*. New York: Academic Press, 1970.

Elaboration

Paivio, A. *Imagery and verbal processes*. New York: Holt, Rinehart & Winston, 1971.

Rohwer, W. D., Jr. Elaboration and learning in childhood and adolescence. In H. W. Reese (Ed.), *Advances in child development and behavior*. Vol. 8. New York: Academic Press, 1973.

Sheehan, P. W. (Ed.) *The function and nature of imagery*. New York: Academic Press, 1972.

Recall of Prose

Hunter, I. M. L. *Memory*. (Rev. ed.) Baltimore: Penguin, 1964. See Chapter IV.

Chapter 6 Verbal Transfer

There are, in general, two sources of transfer in verbal tasks. One source is the association between a stimulus and response as it affects the association between the same stimulus and other responses. The other is *mediation*. We examine both of these in this chapter.

In all the research we will discuss, the experimental task involved is paired-associates. As we saw in Chapter 5, the paired-associate task requires the subject to learn a different response to each of the stimuli in a list. In the transfer designs based on the paired-associate task, the subject must learn a series of lists. The object is to determine how the learning of one list affects the learning or retention of another list when both have the same stimulus items. In other words, the problem is to determine how the learning of one response to a stimulus influences the learning or retention of another response to the same stimulus. We will see that interference usually occurs, but that there are ways to reduce the interference and to obtain facilitation.

Associative Transfer

Associative transfer results from associating different responses with the same stimulus. The transfer is always negative, in the sense that the one association interferes with the other. The transfer is called *associative interference* when the focus is on the learning of a new association. For example, learning the stimulus-response pair *sled-clown* would interfere with learning *sled-cup* later. Presumably, the subject will have trouble with *sled-cup* because he already has learned to respond "clown" when the stimulus word *sled* is presented, and he must unlearn the *sled-clown* association before he can learn the *sled-cup* association.

In spite of associative interference, a subject can eventually learn the new association (*sled-cup* in the example). However, he will usually have some memory of the original association (*sled-clown*). Learning the new association will interfere with this memory, and this interference is called *retroactive interference*. Similarly, because the original association (*sled-clown*) has not been completely forgotten, it will interfere with memory of the new association (*sled-cup*). This interference is called *proactive interference*.

To summarize, associative transfer is called *associative interference* when the interest is in the *learning* of a new association to a stimulus, and is called *retroactive interference* or *proactive interference* when the interest is in the *remembering* of one of the associations to that stimulus. Thus, retroactive and proactive interference are studied after both associations have been *learned*. Retroactive interference means that a newly learned association interferes with memory of a previously learned association to the same stimulus. Proactive interference means that a previously learned association interferes with memory of a newly learned association to the same stimulus.

Associative Interference

Design of the task. In the traditional associative-interference design, two paired-associate lists must be learned. Both have the same stimulus items, but the response items are different. Thus, in one list the subject learns one response to each stimulus; and in the second list the subject must learn a new response to each stimulus. Associative interference means that the new learning is made more difficult by the previous learning.

The experimental demonstration of associative interference requires a comparison condition in which there is no associative transfer. The best comparison condition, or control condition, is to require learning of two lists, each with different stimulus items. Thus, in one list in the control condition the subject learns one response to each stimulus, and in the second list new stimulus items are used, and the subject learns a response to each of these stimuli. There is no associative interference in the control condition, because the stimulus items are not the same in the two lists. By comparing performance in the control condition with performance in the condition described in the preceding paragraph, one can determine whether associative interference occurs, and, if so, how much.

It will simplify our discussion if we use symbols to describe the designs. We can refer to the associative-interference condition as A-B A-C and to the control condition as A-B D-E. These symbols are meant to convey that in the associative-interference condition, the same stimulus (A) occurs in both lists (A-B and A-C) but is associated with a different response in each list (B in List 1 and C in List 2). In the control condition the stimulus in List 2 (D) is not the same as the stimulus in List 1 (A), and each stimulus is associated with a different response (B in List 1 and E in List 2). The symbols will be explained more fully through the example given in the next section.

Sample study. An exemplary study was reported by Spiker (1960, Experiment I). The lists of paired associates used are shown in Table 6.1. As you can see, List 1 consisted of four pairs of words and List 2 consisted of eight pairs of words. Four of the List 2 pairs had the same stimulus words as the List 1 pairs (*cake, sled, drum, train*). The other four List 2 pairs had new stimulus words not appearing in List 1 (*bird, pony, coat, clock*). If the four pairs in List 1 are symbolized as *A-B*, then the first four pairs in List 2 can be symbolized as *A-C* and the last four pairs in List 2 can be symbolized as *D-E*. Thus, the List 1 pairs and the first four List 2 pairs can be symbolized as *A-B A-C*, the associative-interference condition. The List 1 pairs and the last four List 2 pairs can be symbolized as *A-B D-E*, the control condition. By comparing performance on the first four List 2 pairs with performance on the last four List 2 pairs, Spiker was able to assess the amount of associative interference generated by the List 1 learning.

The subjects in Spiker's study were sixth-graders, who were divided into two groups. The groups were given different amounts of training on List 1. One of the groups was

---

Table 6.1
Lists Used by Spiker to Study Associative Interference

List 1		List 2	
Stimulus	*Response*	*Stimulus*	*Response*
cake	boat	cake	fish
sled	clown	sled	cup
drum	tent	drum	bell
train	nest	train	dog
		bird	swing
		pony	kite
		coat	bus
		clock	chair

From Spiker, C. C. Associative transfer in verbal paired-associate learning, *Child Development,* 1960, 31, Table 1, p. 71. Copyright 1960 by the Society for Research in Child Development, Inc. Reprinted by permission.

---

given 6 presentations of List 1, and the other was given 15 presentations of List 1. Following the 6 or 15 presentations of List 1, the subjects were given 12 presentations of List 2. In the different presentations of each list, the pairs were given in different sequences to prevent learning of the response words in serial order, thereby ensuring that correct responses reflected stimulus-response associations.

The results of the study are presented in Figure 6.1. The figure shows the average percentage correct responses to the associative-interference stimuli in List 2 (*cake, sled, drum,*

Figure 6.1
Associative interference in Spiker's study. The amount of interference is reflected by the difference between the curve for the associative-interference condition (solid line) and the curve for the control condition (broken line).

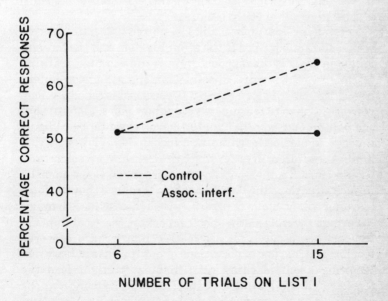

Data points estimated from Spiker, C. C. Associative transfer in verbal paired-associate learning. *Child Development,* 1960, 31, Fig. 1, p. 76.

train) and to the control stimuli in List 2 (*bird, pony, coat, clock*). You can see that when 6 trials were given on List 1, there was no difference between the interference and control conditions in List 2. In other words 6 trials on List 1 did not produce enough learning to generate associative interference with List 2 learning. However, when 15 trials were given on List 1, the List 2 performance in the control condition was considerably better than in the associative-interference condition. Thus, 15 trials on List 1 generated associative interference with List 2 learning.

Implications.   The study shows that when the early material is not well-learned, there is no interference with later learning. A practical implication is that in situations resembling the associative-interference situation, the interference can be avoided if the earlier material is not well-learned. An example of such a situation would be attempting to learn a vocabulary in another language.

Vocabulary learning is like a paired-associate task in which an English word is the stimulus item and the foreign-language word is the response item. As an example, learning Spanish would involve learning, among other vocabulary items, the pair *mother-madre*. If you then studied French, you would have to learn new vocabulary pairs, among them the pair *mother-mère*. The later learning would be difficult unless the earlier learning was incomplete. However, this implication—that in order to learn French more easily, you should learn Spanish poorly—is impractical. Consequently, in such situations the best you can do is realize that the later learning will be made more difficult by the earlier learning.

Perhaps, therefore, the most important practical implication of the research on associative interference concerns teacher and learner expectations about the ease of learning. Knowing about learning set (Chapter 4) might lead the teacher and the learner to expect that performance on the second task will be more efficient than on the first task. But knowing about associative interference warns them that this positive effect is not always obtained, and that the second-task performance may turn out to be *less* efficient. Both should be delighted when it turns out to be more efficient, but neither should be discouraged or dismayed when it turns out to be less so.

Retroactive and Proactive Interference

Design of the tasks. Retroactive and proactive interference are studied with the same kind of interference condition that is used for studying associative interference. Therefore, the interference condition again can be symbolized *A-B A-C*. However, associative interference is interference with *learning* the new list, and retroactive and proactive interference refer to *remembering*. Retroactive interference is interference with remembering the first list; proactive interference is interference with remembering the second list. It follows that the *A-B D-E* control condition needed for assessment of associative interference is more complicated than that needed for assessment of retroactive and proactive interference. The latter refer to what happens to memory *after* learning has occurred, and therefore the only control condition needed is one in which the list to be remembered is learned and interference lists are not learned.

The control condition and the interference conditions used in studies of retroactive and proactive interference are shown in Table 6.2. From the table you can see that the procedure for the retroactive interference condition is: first, learn the *A-B* list; then learn the *A-C* list; then remember the *A-B* list. The more recent learning (*A-C* list) is interpolated between the original learning (*A-B* list) and the memory test (*A-B* list). The interpolated learning interferes with memory for the original learning. In the proactive interference condition the subject learns the same two lists as in the retroactive interference condition but is asked to remember the *A-C* list. The prior learning (*A-B* list) interferes with memory for the more recent learning (*A-C* list).

Sample study. An example is a study by Koppenaal,

Krull, and Katz (1964, Experiment 1), which is one of the few modern studies of retroactive and proactive interference in children. In this experiment the reseachers were interested in age differences in the amounts of retroactive and proactive interference. They tested children, four, five, and eight years old, with a 24-hour interval between the learning phase and the retention test. The reason they selected these ages and this retention interval is that they wanted to test a theory which, together with normative data on language development, predicted that if the retention interval is long, the amounts of retroactive and proactive interference should be greater in eight-year-olds than in four-year-olds (see Koppenaal *et al.* for details).

The materials used were pictures of objects that are easily named by children of the selected ages. The pictures were divided into two lists, each with four pairs of pictures. The lists were of the types symbolized as *A-B* and *A-C*, that is, both had the same stimuli but different responses. Control subjects were given a single list, either the *A-B* list or the *A-C* list.

The procedure for the interference groups involved teaching each subject the two lists, first one and then the other. Twenty-four hours later each child was brought back and tested for recall of either the List 1 responses (retroactive interference) or the List 2 responses (proactive interference).

Table 6.2
Design for Assessing Retroactive and Proactive Interference

| | | Phase | |
Condition	Learn	Learn	Recall
Interference			
Retroactive	A-B	A-C	A-B
Proactive	A-B	A-C	A-C
Control	—	A-C	A-C

Adapted from Underwood, B. J. *Experimental psychology: An introduction.* 1949, table on p. 544. Copyright 1949 by Prentice-Hall, Inc. Used by permission of Prentice-Hall, Inc.

In the control condition the subjects learned one list and were tested for recall of it 24 hours later.

Figure 6.2 shows the results of this experiment. The data

Figure 6.2
Retroactive and proactive interference at three age levels. The data points are corrected for performance in a control, no-interference condition. Hence, the higher the score, the greater the interference. (The measure of interference is a ratio: the mean number of correct responses for the control group minus the mean for an interference group, divided by the mean for the control group.)

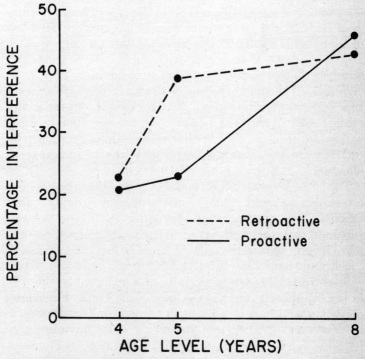

Drawn from data presented by Koppenaal, R. J.,Krull, A., and Katz, H. Age, interference, and forgetting, *Journal of Experimental Child Psychology*, 1964, 1, Table 2, p. 365.

points in the figure reflect the extent, expressed as a percentage, to which each interference group was inferior to the control group (see Underwood, 1949, p. 545). The higher the value, the greater the interference. You can see that there was little interference of either kind at four years of age; there was retroactive interference but not much proactive interference at five years; and there was considerable interference of both kinds at eight years. Thus, new learning interfered with memory of old learning (retroactive interference) in the five- and eight-year-olds but not in the four-year-olds. Old learning interfered with memory of new learning (proactive interference) only in the eight-year-olds.

Other research. As we mentioned earlier, there have been few studies of retroactive and proactive interference in children. In contrast, there have been many studies of these phenomena in adults. These, like the study by Koppenaal *et al.*, have shown that retroactive interference is generally stronger than proactive interference. In addition, they have shown that the amount of learning has a strong influence on the amount of interference. Retroactive interference increases with increases in the amount of interpolated learning and in the number of interpolated lists. Similarly, proactive interference increases with increases in the amount of prior learning and in the number of prior lists.

The research with adults has also shown that the amount of retroactive and proactive interference is strongly influenced by the similarity of the material. In the paired-associate task the material is most similar when the same stimuli occur in both lists. There would be less interference if the stimuli were similar but not identical.

Stimuli can be either formally or semantically similar. *Formal similarity* refers to the form of the words. For example, *bat* and *bit* have two letters in common and are therefore more similar formally than *bat* and *big* which have only one letter in common. *Semantic similarity* is similarity of meanings. For example, *bat* and *hit* are more similar in meaning—more similar semantically—than *bat* and *bit*.

Formal similarity seems to produce more interference in younger children, and semantic similarity seems to produce more interference in older children and adults.

Applications. These principles can be put to practical use. The principles imply that errors can be reduced by making new material more distinctively different from old material. The old material will be remembered better (reduction of retroactive interference), and the new material will be remembered better (reduction of proactive interference). To make the new material more distinctively different from the old, it is more important to work with formal similarity in teaching young children and with similarity of meaning in teaching older children.

The principles also have implications that are similar to those for associative interference. For example, the teacher who wants students to know Spanish better than French can teach Spanish first and require that his students learn the Spanish vocabulary well. As noted in the section on associative interference, this learning will make learning the French vocabulary harder. In addition, even if the French vocabulary is learned, it will be harder to remember because of the increased amount of proactive interference from the well-learned Spanish vocabulary.

Imagery and Associative Transfer

We saw in Chapter 5 that paired-associate learning is greatly facilitated by pictorial elaborations and visual images of interactions between the stimulus and response items in a pair. That is, pictorial elaborations and visual images make stimulus-response associations easy to learn. In addition, once the associations are learned, these elaborations make them easy to remember, at least for a few days. Thus, the elaborations are not only effective as learning aids but also as short-term memory aids or *mnemonic devices*. It has also been found that visual images reduce the kinds of interference identified as associative transfer.

Imagery and associative interference. The effect of visual images on associative interference can be seen in an experiment by Spiker (1960, Experiment III). The procedure was the same as in Spiker's study described earlier in the section on associative interference, with two exceptions. First, all subjects were given nine presentations of List 1. Second, after the second presentation of List 1 the apparatus was shut off and further instructions were given. Each subject in a "noninstructed" group was reminded about the experimental procedure but was told nothing about mnemonic devices. Each subject in an "imagery" group was told that the experimenter

> was going to tell him a trick that would help him learn the list. The experimenter then illustrated a mnemonic device for each of the four pairs in List 1. The subject was instructed to visualize a "cake-boat," that is, a boat made of cake; a clown riding on a sled; someone playing a drum in a tent; etc. . . . . Following the presentation of List 1, the experimenter suggested that the trick had helped and that during the next list the subject should invent his own devices (Spiker, 1960, p. 81).

The results of the study are shown graphically in Figure 6.3. The measure used is the same as in Figure 6.2: the data points reflect the percentage by which the interference condition was inferior to the control condition. The figure shows that on the first two trials associative interference was greater in the imagery group, and on the last four trials it was greater in the noninstructed group. In between there was no difference between the groups in the amount of interference. Apparently imagery may produce a quick increase in associative interference, but with further training imagery eliminates associative interference.

A practical application of this effect of imagery might be found in learning foreign-language vocabularies. For example, consider a student who is going to learn French after having learned Spanish. He can use visual imagery in learning the vocabularies, which should make learning the French vocabulary easier. To learn the foreign-language word for *mother*, he might use an image of a woman holding a baby to represent the word *mother*. He could then relate the word *madre* to this woman dressed in the Spanish style, and later relate the word *mère* to this woman dressed in high French fashion.

Other than Spiker's study there has been little research with children on the effects of imagery on associative interference. Furthermore, there has been little work with adults. What research has been done supports Spiker's findings, except that there is some indication that in adults imagery may reduce associative interference from the very beginning of training on the second list instead of after the first few trials on the second list.

Figure 6.3

Effect of imagery on associative interference. The higher the score, the greater the interference. Zero indicates no interference. (The scores are corrected for performance in a control, no-interference condition, using the measure of interference defined in the caption of Figure 6.2.)

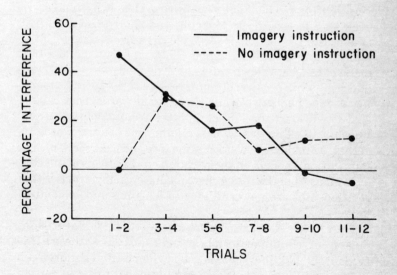

Drawn from data estimated from Spiker, C. C. Associative transfer in verbal paired-associate learning. *Child Development,* 1960, 31, Fig. 3, p. 82.

Imagery and retroactive–proactive interference. There has been no research with children on the effects of imagery on retroactive and proactive interference, and there has been very little with adults. The research with adults suggests that imagery reduces retroactive interference and may reduce proactive interference. The practical implications for memory tasks are analogous to the implications of associative interference for learning tasks.

As we saw in Chapter 5 in the section on elaboration in paired-associate learning, there is conflicting evidence about the effect of imagery on long-term retention. There is reason to believe that imagery may be less effective for long-term retention—over several weeks or months—than verbal elaboration. Consequently, the reduction of interference by imagery is likely to be most effective for the *learning* of material and for short-term *retention* of the material. Imagery can make the learning easier but may need to be bolstered by verbal training to yield a high level of long-term retention.

Implications. It is not yet entirely clear why imagery is such an effective aid to learning and short-term retention. One possibility is that it serves to organize the material by making interrelations explicit. That is, an image of a boat made of cake or a clown riding on a sled may be easy to learn and remember because it requires the subject to find a meaningful relation between the two critical words, boat-cake or sled-clown. Once the subject finds that relationship, the relationship itself serves as a mediator linking the words together, as in mediated association (see the next section). The implication, then, from the research on the effects of imagery (as well as from the research on mediated association) is that relationships are powerful aids to learning and remembering.

The teacher should therefore attempt to find relationships among curriculum materials or facts and convey these to the student. In addition, there is good evidence that children can be taught to devise their own visual images to aid in paired-associate learning and transfer. Consequently, the teacher should attempt to teach students to look for relatedness in course contents because such relationships will aid learning and remembering. The implication, then, is two-fold: teachers should show students how materials are related and should teach students to look for relationships among materials to be learned or remembered. The relationships should be made as distinctive as possible to minimize associative transfer and thereby interference.

Mediated Transfer

We discussed the concept of mediation in Chapter 4 (see Figure 4.2, p. 71). Briefly, it refers to a kind of chaining in which the initial stimulus arouses a response (the mediator) which produces a stimulus (the mediating stimulus) which in turn arouses the terminal response. In verbal learning, mediation can produce positive or negative transfer, depending on the experimental situation. That is, with one arrangement of the materials, mediation facilitates new learning; and with another arrangement, mediation interferes with new learning.

The experimental designs. The experimental demonstration of mediated transfer in paired-associate tasks requires the learning of three lists of word-pairs. Mediated transfer is analogous to the syllogism in logic. For example, the syllogism might be:

Major premise:
This object is a dog.
Minor premise:
Dogs bite.
Conclusion:
This object bites.

The corresponding paired associates are:

List 1 pair:
object—dog
List 2 pair:
dog—bite
List 3 pair:
object—bite.

As a result of learning Lists 1 and 2, the List 3 learning should be easy. In symbols the three lists can be represented as A-B, B-C, A-C. Mediated transfer, or mediated association, means that in List 3 the stimulus word, A, arouses subvocally the response word, B, which was associated with A in List 1. The word B, in turn, arouses the response word C, which was associated with B in List 2. Since C is the correct response to A in List 3, the learning of the A-C association should be easy.

Mediated associations can facilitate List 3 performance or interfere with it. Table 6.3 shows sample materials for mediated facilitation, mediated interference, and control conditions. Each condition includes three lists of word pairs. A subject learns all three lists in a condition, and different subjects are used in the different conditions. The top section of the table shows three lists for the study of mediated facilitation. If mediation occurs in List 3 the stimulus word *cake*, for example, will arouse the mediating word *boat*, learned in List 1, which as a result of List 2 learning will arouse *fish*, the correct response to *cake* in List 3. The middle section of the table shows an arrangement for the study of mediated interference. You can see that if mediation occurs it will produce the wrong response to the stimulus word in List 3. The bottom section of the table shows a typical control condition. The control condition can be symbolized A-B, D-C, A-C. No mediation can occur because no association has been learned between B and C. The conditions differ only with respect to the pairs in List 2. Lists 1 and 3 are the same in all conditions.

Sample study. A classic example is a study by Norcross and Spiker (1958, Experiment I). They used the design shown in Table 6.3, except that the materials were pictures of objects readily named by the subjects. The subjects were kindergarteners. Each subject was given three lists, like those shown in Table 6.3. Each list included pairs representing all three experimental conditions (see Norcross and Spiker, 1958, for details). The subjects were trained to a learning criterion of two runs through List 1 with all responses correct. The sequence of pairs in each presentation of the list was varied so that the responses would not be learned in serial order.

The procedure was to present a stimulus word, wait a few seconds for the subject to give a response, and then present the stimulus word together with the correct response word to show the subject what his response should have been. On the second experimental day, which followed learning of List 1, the subjects learned List 2 in the same way. Finally, on the third experimental day, Lists 1 and 2 were relearned to criterion and, after a brief rest period, List 3 was presented five times for learning.

The critical data are the correct responses in the five presentations of List 3. The percentage correct responses in these trials were 74 percent for the mediated facilitation condition, 48 percent for the control condition, and 44 percent for the mediated interference condition. The percentage facilitation in the mediated facilitation condition (calculated as in Figure 6.2) was 53 percent. The percentage interference in the mediated interference condition was only 9 percent.

Table 6.3
Sample of Materials for Assessing Mediated Transfer

Condition	List 1	List 2	List 3
Mediated Facilitation	cake——boat	boat——fish	cake—— fish
	sled——clown	clown—cup	sled—— cup
	drum—tent	tent——bell	drum— bell
	train—nest	nest——dog	train— dog
Mediated Interference	cake——boat	boat——cup	cake—— fish
	sled——clown	clown—fish	sled—— cup
	drum—tent	tent——dog	drum— bell
	train— nest	nest——bell	train— dog
Control	cake——boat	bird——fish	cake—— fish
	sled——clown	pony——cup	sled—— cup
	drum—tent	coat——bell	drum— bell
	train—nest	clock——dog	train— dog

Thus, the amount of mediated facilitation was large, but the amount of mediated interference was negligible. This finding is fairly common in research with children. It is much easier to obtain mediated facilitation than to obtain mediated interference. One interpretation of this finding is that children suppress the mediator when it begins to produce interference and continue to use it when it produces facilitation.

Norcross and Spiker (1958, Experiment II) repeated the experiment with first-graders and with only the mediated interference and control conditions. By increasing the number of pairs in these conditions—accomplished by substituting interference and control pairs for the mediated-facilitation pairs—they succeeded in obtaining a more precise estimate of mediated interference. The percentage of correct responses was 41 percent in the interference condition and 52 percent in the control condition. The percentage interference was 21 percent. Although the percentages of correct responses for the interference and control groups were fairly similar to the percentages obtained in their first experiment, the percentage interference was considerably greater.

Other research. Nikkel and Palermo (1965) tested sixth-graders in an experiment similar to Norcross and Spiker's first experiment. The main results showed that there was significant facilitation in the mediated-facilitation condition and significant interference in the mediated-interference condition. In addition, Nikkel and Palermo analyzed the numbers of *mediated errors* in the mediated-interference condition. An example of a mediated error can be taken from Table 6.3. In List 1 the subject learns *cake-boat*; in List 2 he learns *boat-cup*; and in List 3, in the mediated-interference condition, he is supposed to learn *cake-fish*. If mediation occurs in List 3, *cake* arouses the mediating response *boat*, and *boat* arouses *cup*. Thus, since *fish* is the correct List 3 response, the mediated response, *cup*, is an error—a mediated error. Nikkel and Palermo found that the number of mediated errors was much greater than would be expected to occur by chance. This finding provides strong support for the theory that the poor performance in the interference condition results from mediation of incorrect response items.

Mediation can have a powerful influence on paired-associate learning when the materials are arranged appropriately. There is some evidence that it may not be as effective for young children as for older children and adults, but the impact of this evidence is offset by other evidence that special training can make mediation effective even for young children.

Implications.   The first two lists in studies of mediated association can be seen as establishing relationships among materials. That is, the *A-B* and *B-C* learning establishes a relationship between *A* and *C*, mediated by *B*. By implication, then, establishing relationships among materials should generally make learning easier. In practical situations, such as classroom learning, it should be better to make interrelations explicit than to let the student discover them or not, depending on his insights. That is, it should be better to tell the student what the relationships are instead of relying on the student to find them for himself. You may have noticed that we have made practical use of this implication in this textbook. We have done this by showing how basic learning situations are *related* to real-life situations in order to suggest implications of the basic research.

Summary of Verbal Transfer

Transfer of verbal learning results from the association between a stimulus and response, as it affects the association between that stimulus and another response; or it results from mediation. The first kind of transfer is always interference; the second kind can be interference or facilitation.

Associative interference.   Associative interference

means that learning a response to a stimulus interferes with later learning of a new response to the same stimulus. The amount of associative interference increases as the first stimulus-response association increases in strength. That is, more strongly learned pairings produce more associative interference. When the first pairing is poorly learned, it may produce no interference at all.

Retroactive and proactive interference. Retroactive interference means that after learning a response to a stimulus, learning a new response to the same stimulus interferes with later recall of the original response. That is, new learning interferes with *memory* for old learning. Proactive interference means that the old learning interferes with *memory* for the new learning.

In young preschoolers there is not much interference of either kind, but in older children there is considerable interference of both kinds. In between, there is more retroactive interference than proactive interference. These data, which are from one study, are not entirely consistent with data from studies with adults, which generally show more retroactive than proactive interference.

Retroactive interference increases as the amount of interpolated learning increases; and proactive interference increases as the amount of prior learning increases. Both also increase with increases in the similarity of the materials in the two learning phases.

Imagery and associative transfer. When children use imagery to learn the stimulus-response associations in a paired-associate list, there is an increase in associative interference. However, the interference quickly disappears and imagery subsequently improves performance. There is some evidence that in adults imagery eliminates associative interference altogether.

The effect of imagery on retroactive and proactive interference in children has never been studied. Studies with adults suggest that imagery reduces both of these kinds of interference, but the effect may be limited to relatively short retention intervals. Long-term memory may not be affected by imagery (see Chapter 5). It is not clear why imagery is effective. It is possible that it serves to organize the material by making interrelations explicit. Organized material is easier to learn and remember than unorganized material.

Mediated transfer. We discussed two kinds of mediated transfer: mediated facilitation and mediated interference. In mediated facilitation a stimulus arouses a mediator which produces a response that is appropriate for the stimulus. In mediated interference the mediator produces a response that is inappropriate for the stimulus. The appropriateness or inappropriateness of the mediated response is determined by the arrangement of the materials. Mediated transfer may occur because of the establishment of relationships among materials.

Mediated facilitation is more effective in facilitating performance than mediated interference is in interfering with performance, particularly in children. Perhaps children suppress the mediator when it begins to produce interference.

Suggested Readings

General

Goulet, L. R. Verbal learning in children: Implications for developmental research. *Psychological Bulletin,* 1968, *69*, 359-376.

Keppel, G. Verbal learning in children. *Psychological Bulletin,* 1964, *61*, 63-80.

Palermo, D. S. Transfer in paired-associate tasks. In H. W. Reese & L. P. Lipsitt (Eds.), *Experimental child psychology.* New York: Academic Press, 1970. Pp. 250-257.

Imagery and Transfer

Paivio, A. *Imagery and verbal processes.* New York: Holt, Rinehart and Winston, 1971.

Chapter 7 Conceptual Processes

Conceptual processes include the learning and utilization of concepts. A particular *concept* refers to a class of phenomena that differ from phenomena not in that class. In other words, the phenomena that are members of a particular conceptual class are so because they differ from other phenomena not in that class. The differentiating characteristic is that the members of the class share a set of attributes that are not shared by nonmembers. A simple example is the concept of redness. All red objects are *red*—they belong to the class of red objects—because they share the attribute of redness, which is not possessed by objects that are not red—objects that are not in this class

Concept learning. A particular conceptual class may or may not have a name. However, all conceptual classes that interest humans have been given names. In studies of concept attainment one procedure is to teach a name for a conceptual class. If the subject can apply this name consistently and correctly, then he has demonstrated that he knows the conceptual class, that he knows the *meaning* of the concept name. Another procedure is to require that a subject make a motor response—pointing to an object, for example—whenever the name of a conceptual class is presented. If he makes this response consistently and correctly, then again it is demonstrated that he knows the conceptual class. Actually, there is no essential difference between the procedures. Both require the subject to make some kind of instrumental response—verbal or motor—to all members of the conceptual class and to withhold this response from all nonmembers.

Concept utilization. Once acquired, concepts can be used in several ways. We have already considered one of these, the use of concepts as mediating responses, in Chapters 4 and 6. In this chapter we will look at two other uses.

One way concepts can be used is as devices for coding visual information. As such, they can affect memory, for better or worse depending on the accuracy or relevance of the coding. For example, the drawing in Figure 7.1 could be coded as a "fir tree." Memory might be improved if the drawing is actually intended to represent a fir tree, but not if it is intended to represent an arrowhead.

A concept can also be used as a general controlling device or "set." For example, a person who has been viewing drawings representing various kinds of trees is likely to see the Figure 7.1 drawing as a tree, and a person who has been viewing Indian scenes is likely to see it as an arrowhead. The expectation or set to see particular kinds of drawings is established if the person notices that the preliminary drawings are all members of one conceptual class.

Concept Attainment

Concept identification and concept formation. In studies of concept attainment the concept may already be known to the subject, or it may be entirely new. If it is already known, concept *identification* is being studied. The subject who already knows the conceptual class does not need to learn or form the concept; all he needs to do is identify which of his concepts is the one the experimenter wants him to apply or to name. In contrast, if the conceptual class is not

Figure 7.1
Memory for this drawing may be influenced by the way it is labeled or by what other pictures a subject has been shown.

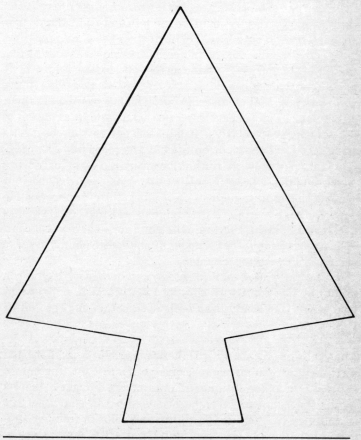

already known to the subject, then concept *formation* is involved.

In adults it is likely that all important concrete conceptual classes are already known. There are abstract conceptual classes unknown to many adults, and learning these would be concept formation. But, if we wish to do research on the formation of concrete concepts, we must study the process in children, who have a limited repertoire of conceptual classes.

Consider the concept of left and right. Many four-year-old children cannot identify their left and right hands, but most five-year-olds can. However, until the age of about eight the child cannot correctly identify the left and right hands of a person who is facing him. Up until then the child identifies left and right on a mirror-image basis. That is, he identifies the facing person's right hand as the left because his own left hand is on the same side in absolute space. Thus the young child has a concept of left and right which is based on his own orientation as an observer. In contrast, the adult's concept of left and right is relative. It is based not on the observer's orientation but on the orientation of the referents. The progress of the child toward the adult concept is a result of concept formation, not concept identification. The progress does not require the child to identify new labels for old concepts. He does not learn merely to switch labels, calling "left" what he used to call "right." Rather, the child forms a new concept. When the concept of left and right changes from absolute to relative, its *meaning* changes.

Most of the experimental research, whether with children or adults, has dealt with concept identification, not concept formation. One study that dealt with both was reported by Hollenberg (1970).

The Hollenberg study. Hollenberg (1970) was interested in the effect of imagery on concept attainment. Instead of using the usual techniques to manipulate imagery such as instructions or pictorial elaborations, she defined imagery as an individual-difference or ability variable. To find her subjects, she gave 380 children from Grades 1 to 4 a battery of tests intended to measure their visual-imagery ability. Children whose scores were in the highest 25 percent were matched for sex, IQ, and grade with children whose scores were in the lowest 25 percent. The result was a total of 32 children who had strong visual imagery, each of whom was matched with a child low in visual-imagery ability.

The stimuli in Hollenberg's study were line drawings, divided into four categories of ten drawings each. The categories were foods, toys, "creature A," and "creature B." The foods were pear, ice cream cone, loaf of bread, cherries, etc. The toys were blocks, baseball and bat, horn, tennis racket, sailboat, etc. The creatures were "modeled after those of Dr. Seuss" (p. 1006). Creature A "had a small head (with a skinny neck), a wide bottom, and no arms. Creature B had a fat head (with no neck), a skinny bottom, and possessed arms or some similar appendage" (p. 1006).

The procedure consisted of presenting one figure from each category and teaching a different nonsense-syllable name for each figure. Then another figure from each category was presented, and the child was asked to guess the name of each one. After the child guessed, he was taught the nonsense-syllable names, using the same name for each category as in the first set of figures. The procedure continued until the child guessed the names correctly three times in a row, with new figures each time, or until all the figures had been used.

The learning involving toys and foods required concept identification. Suppose, as an example, that the nonsense-name *nad* was the label for the drawing of the blocks in the first set of four figures and also for the horn in the second set. If, in the third set, the child guessed "nad" for the picture of the tennis racket, then the child must have inferred that *nad* is the name of the toys. He already had the concept of toys, presumably, and merely had to learn to say "nad" instead of saying "toys." He had to identify which of the concepts he already knew, including the concept of toys, was associated with the new name *nad*.

In contrast, the learning involving the two kinds of nonsense creatures required concept formation. The child had no pre-formed concepts of creatures like these, and therefore he had to form concepts in order to be able to guess the correct labels for new examples of the concepts.

Hollenberg's results. Hollenberg found that concept attainment was easier with the toys and foods than with the two kinds of nonsense creatures. In other words, concept identification was easier than concept formation in this study. Hollenberg also found that concept attainment of both kinds was easier for the children who were low in imagery ability than for those high in this ability. This finding is especially remarkable because the low imagery children were *inferior* to the high-imagery children in the name-learning phase of the study. The low-imagery children required an average of 33 percent more trials than the high-imagery children to learn the names for the first set of four figures. In other words, learning names for specific figures was harder for children with low-imagery ability. However, learning that certain figures were related to each other and had the same name was easier for these children.

Apparently children who rely on visual imagery in thinking are not as efficient in concept attainment as children who rely on words. It may be that visual images are so rich in details that common characteristics are hard to detect. There is some experimental evidence to support this suggestion (see Tighe, Schechter, & Tighe, 1973, and the discussion of this study later in this chapter). If this suggestion is correct, then the Hollenberg study identifies a limit on the usefulness of imagery. That is, imagery is useful for learning and remembering specific facts (Chapter 5) and for reducing interference with learning and remembering conflicting facts (Chapter 6). However, imagery seems to be detrimental when the task requires that individual details be ignored, as in concept attainment.

Unanswered questions. Unfortunately, there have been no other studies of the effects of imagery on concept attainment. It would be useful to find out whether the negative effect of imagery is general in concept attainment or is limited to concepts like those studied by Hollenberg. Would imagery interfere with identification of less abstract concepts than foods and toys? Would it interfere, for example, with identification of the more concrete concepts of fruits and "things to ride in"? (The latter are more concrete than foods and toys because they are subcategories under the general concepts of foods and toys.) Further, would imagery interfere with the formation of more meaningful concepts than nonsense creatures? One additional problem involves the finding that concept identification with foods and toys was easier than concept formation with nonsense creatures. Is concept identification inherently easier than concept formation, or does it depend on the nature of the concepts? Though at present there are no answers to these questions, future research may be able to supply solutions.

Developmental trends.   Hollenberg found that concept attainment was faster in the older children. This finding, that older children can form and identify concepts more rapidly than younger children, has been obtained in a large number of studies. However, we should emphasize that these have been studies in which the same concept is taught at different ages. Consequently, there may be a limitation on the practical implication, because in school situations older children are generally required to learn much more difficult concepts than younger children. Thus the older child may not have as hard a time as the younger child in learning a particular concept. But the older child may have as much trouble learning the concepts he is required to learn in school as the younger child has in learning the simpler concepts *he* is required to learn.

Theoretical analysis.   Concept formation requires analyzing stimuli (or facts) and finding common attributes. In order for a child to form a concept, he must be able to identify the attributes that define the conceptual class. The problem in concept identification is similar in that the child needs to find the common characteristics. However, this task may be easier because he has a stockpile of such common characteristics already categorized, which he can try out to see if any works. In concept identification the child can try to outguess the experimenter by applying concepts. When he finds the appropriate one, the task is solved. Apparently in concept formation the child begins with the same approach—trying out concepts. When he discovers that none of his concepts is appropriate, he must look for the common characteristic or attribute that underlies the unknown concept. Theoretically, then, concept formation should be more difficult than concept identification.

This analysis of concept attainment has implications for the reasons why older children can form and identify concepts more quickly than younger children. First, the child must analyze the stimuli. To do so, he must attend to attributes and not to the whole stimulus as such. As already mentioned, this requirement may be why imagery interferes with concept attainment. The young child is known to be less attentive to stimulus attributes than the older child and to be less systematic in looking at attributes. The studies of the effects of attention on discriminative learning which were discussed in Chapter 3 demonstrate this fact. The child must also abandon false leads. We know from the discussion of research on learning sets (Chapter 4) that older children give up false leads more readily than younger children. Finally, the child must produce the concept in order to demonstrate that he has attained it. In Chapters 4 and 6 we saw that younger children are less likely than older children to produce concepts. For all these reasons, and perhaps for others, concept attainment should be harder for the younger child.

Concepts as Mediators

In Chapters 4 and 6 we discussed the use of concepts as mediating responses. We mention this use here only as a reminder. Whenever a person uses a concept name to label an object or event and then responds to the label rather than to the object or event per se, he is using the concept as a mediator. As we mentioned in Chapter 4, a real-life example is stereotyping. Stereotyping can have socially desirable or undesirable consequences, depending on the nature of the responses mediated by the label.

Concepts as Codes

Coding. The *coding* use of concepts is similar to the mediation use in that both involve using concept names as labels for objects or events. However, in mediation the label elicits further responses that have been conditioned to the label, while in coding the label serves only as a memory device.

The coding use of concepts has been found to affect both reproductive memory and recognition memory. In reproductive memory the subject must draw or reconstruct the items that were shown. In recognition memory he must select from an array of items those that were shown before.

Coding and reproductive memory. The best-known example of the use of concept names as codes for reproductive memory is a study by Carmichael, Hogan, and Walter (1932). The subjects, who were college students, were shown drawings like those in Figure 7.2, one at a time, and each drawing was labeled aloud by the experimenter. The experimenter said, for example, "The next one resembles eyeglasses." For one group of subjects, the labels shown to the left of the drawings were used and for the other group, the labels used were those to the right of the drawings. After all the drawings had been shown and labeled, each subject was asked to reproduce from memory the drawings he had seen. Figure 7.3 shows a sample of the results. As you can see, the subjects tended to make errors in their drawings which related to the labels they had heard.

These general results have been confirmed by other researchers in children as well as adults. Apparently the labels were used as memory aids which influenced the way the

Figure 7.2
Sample of drawings and labels used by Carmichael, Hogan, and Walter. Half of the subjects (Group A) heard the labels shown to the left of the drawings and the other subjects (Group B) heard the labels shown to the right.

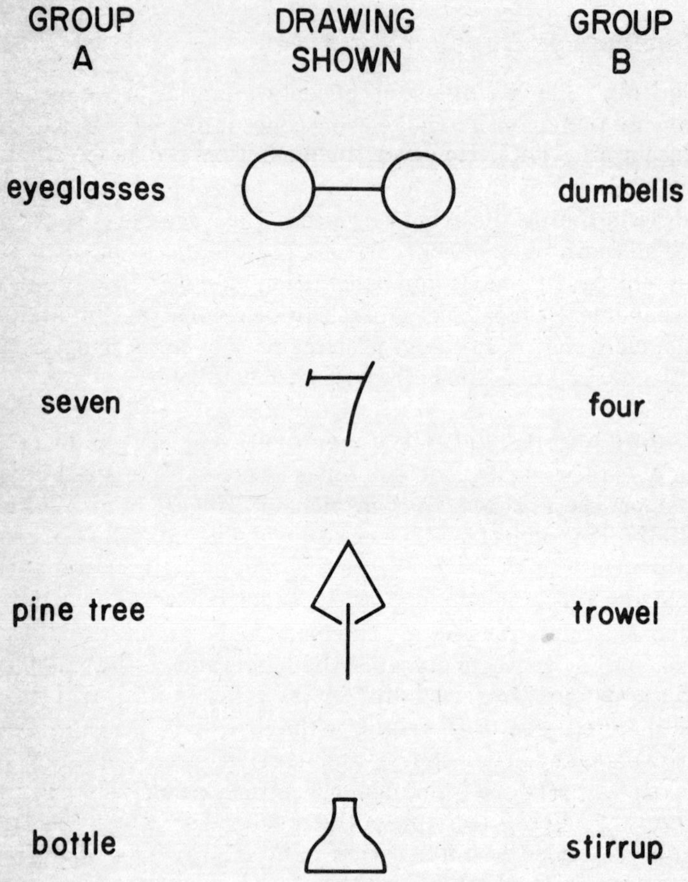

GROUP A	DRAWING SHOWN	GROUP B
eyeglasses		dumbells
seven		four
pine tree		trowel
bottle		stirrup

From Carmichael, L., Hogan, H.P., & Walter, A.A. An experimental study of the effect of language on the reproduction of visually perceived form. *Journal of Experimental Psychology,* 1932, 15, Chart I, p. 75. Copyright 1932 by the American Psychological Association. Used by permission.

Figure 7.3

Sample of reproductions drawn from memory by subjects in the Carmichael, Hogan, and Walter study. Note that the labels influenced the way the drawings were remembered. The experimenters described these samples as "some selected examples of pronounced modifications" (p. 79), but the less pronounced modifications tended to be of the same type.

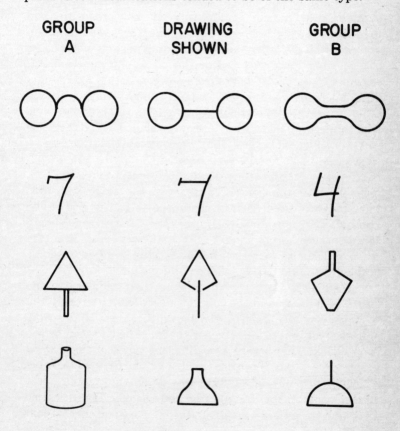

GROUP A   DRAWING SHOWN   GROUP B

From Carmichael, L., Hogan, H. P., & Walter, A. A. An experimental study of the effect of language on the reproduction of visually perceived form. *Journal of Experimental Psychology*, 1932, 15, Chart II, p. 80. Copyright 1932 by the American Psychological Association. Used by permission.

original drawings were remembered. Unfortunately for the subjects, however, memory was inaccurate because the labels were not entirely appropriate for the drawings.

Coding and recognition memory.   A study related to conceptual coding and recognition memory was reported by Tighe, Schechter, and Tighe (1973). Their subjects were seven-year-olds and college students. The materials were 16 printed words. If a child could not read, the words were read to him by the experimenter. Eight of the words were names of animals, and the other eight were names of parts of the body. The subjects' task was to learn to make one instrumental response to the eight words from one conceptual class and a different instrumental response to the eight words from the other conceptual class. The words were presented one at a time, and the subjects were told only to learn which response was correct for each word. They were not told that there was a conceptual basis for the responses.

This aspect of the study dealt with concept identification, not concept formation, because even the seven-year-olds knew the concepts of animal and parts of the body. The results were consistent with other research on concept attainment: the adults made 72 percent fewer errors than the children. Furthermore, all but one of the adults solved the problem, while only two of the children solved it.

The subjects were also tested for their memory of the specific words used in the concept-identification task. In the memory test each subject was shown three words at a time and was required to tell which of the three he had seen before in the task. There were five different types of three-word groups presented. These are illustrated and defined in Table 7.1. One subgroup of subjects was given the memory test immediately after completing the concept-identification task, and the others were given the memory test three weeks later.

Immediate recognition.   In the immediate test there were almost no errors by either age group on the three-word groups that included a correct word—that is, on Types 1 through 4. However, in Type 5 word groups, the words that represented a conceptual class from the original list were selected 94 percent of the time by the adults and only 50 percent of time by the children. This result suggests that the adults were using the names of the conceptual classes as memory aids. They remembered that they had seen body parts, for example, and therefore chose *neck* in the Type 5 sample shown in Table 7.1, even though *neck* was not in the original list. This tendency to respond conceptually was an aid in the concept-identification phase of the study but was a hindrance in the memory phase.

Delayed recognition.   In the delayed memory test there were relatively few errors on Types 1 through 4, as shown in Table 7.2. The children made similar percentages of errors on

---

Table 7.1
Types of Word Arrays Used by Tighe, Schechter, and Tighe (1973) in Memory Test

Type	Sample Array[1]	Description
1	bear, apple, door	The incorrect choices, or "ringers," are from conceptual classes not in the original list.
2	dog, cat, car	One ringer from same class as correct word; other ringer from class not in original list.
3	arm, nose, farm	Same as Type 2, except that ringer from new class rhymes with correct word.
4	fox, snake, tiger	Both ringers from same class as correct word.
5	neck, peach, belt	Same as Type 1, except that the first word is also a ringer.[2]

[1]The first word listed in the sample of each type is the correct one. In the actual test the correct word could be in the left, middle, or right position.

[2]In Type 5 there is no correct choice. All three words are ringers, but one of them (the first one listed) is from a conceptual class represented in the original list.

all types. In contrast, the adults made more errors, the greater the number of ringers (wrong words) there were that represented the same conceptual class as the correct word. On Type 5 word groups, for which only errors were possible, the ringer representing a conceptual class from the original list was chosen all of the time by the adults and only 60 percent of the time by the children. These results confirm the suggestion from the immediate memory test: the adults were using the concept names as memory aids. The children made fewer errors because the memory test required remembering specific words. They tended to remember the specific words, while the adults were sometimes confused because they remembered the concepts and not the specific words. Put another way, the children tended more to remember specific meanings, and the adults tended more to remember general meanings (that is, conceptual meanings).

Implications. In general, adults tend to use cognitive short cuts more than children. In the Tighe, Schechter, and Tighe study, this tendency was demonstrated by the adults' remembering the conceptual classes, which aided them in the concept-identification phase but hindered them in the memory task.

These trends can be capitalized on by a teacher. If specifics are to be remembered, the adult must be discouraged somehow from generalizing; and if generalities are to be remem-

Table 7.2
Percentage Errors on Delayed Memory Test

| Age Group | *Array Type* | | |
	1	*2 & 3*	*4*
Child	5.0	9.4	8.1
Adult	0	11.8	17.8

Note: Types 2 and 3 are combined because both have one ringer from the same class as the correct word and one from a new class (see Table 7.1). (Adapted from Tighe *et al.*, 1973, Table 2.)

bered, the child must be encouraged somehow to generalize. Instruction about the task requirements will probably be sufficient to discourage generalizing in the adult. For the child, a concept-identification task could be used to encourage generalizing, but training would need to continue until the child succeeded in identifying the relevant concepts.

Concepts as Sets

The *setting* use of concepts differs from the mediation and coding uses in being more general or diffuse in its effects. The studies in this area fall into several categories, including *functional fixedness*, *insight*, *perceptual set*, and *cognitive set*.

Functional fixedness   In functional fixedness a person focuses so strongly on the standard function or use of an object that he cannot find a new function for it. His concept of pliers, for example, may so strongly incorporate the notion of grasping or pinching that he cannot extend the concept to include the function of a pendulum. The usual textbook example of this is Maier's (1931) two-string problem. In this experiment two strings are suspended from the ceiling far enough apart that the subject cannot hold one and reach the other. His task is to tie the ends together. Among other objects in the room are pliers. The solution requires the subject to tie the pliers to the end of one string and to swing them so that when he holds the end of the other string he can catch the swinging one and then tie the ends together.

Functional fixedness results from a rigid and narrow application of concepts. Problems related to functional fixedness are often included in tests of creativity. A high score, presumably reflecting high creative ability, is achieved by thinking up a large number of alternative uses for a common object. In other words, creativity implies an ability to overcome functional fixedness. For example, the subject might be asked to think up new uses for a coat hanger or a brick. The scoring on such tests is based on the total number of new uses mentioned and on the quality of the new uses. Quality means that the new use is unusual and possible. In general, there is an increase in performance levels with increasing age in childhood. It appears, therefore, that creative ability, like other intellectual processes, improves with increasing age.

Insight. Insight is the sudden solution of a problem as a result of reorganizing or recombining previous experiences. Insight is obviously related to the functional-fixedness problems. For example, Maier's two-string problem requires combining previous experience with pendulums and previous experience with weights including pliers.

Kendler and Kendler (1967) reviewed animal and child research on insight and discussed their own research with children. The Kendlers distinguished between two kinds of "insight." In one the subject must choose "from among two or more previously connected behavior sequences the one that is appropriate to a newly introduced motivation-reinforcement contingency" (p. 172). In other words, the previous experiences have already been integrated into separate behavioral units, and the subject needs only to choose the one that is appropriate to the task. This kind of insight is analogous to concept identification. In the other kind of insight, the subject must integrate previous experiences that have not before been integrated. Previously learned behaviors must be combined in a novel way.

The Kendlers' review showed that rats and young children are capable of the first kind of insight. However, rats and very young children cannot achieve the second kind of insight, although this kind does develop in children as they grow older. It is this second kind of insight that most psychologists would call "real" insight. It can therefore be concluded that true insight—truly insightful problem-solving—increases with increasing age. According to the Kendlers, this kind of insight is related to "representational responses," which in humans are likely to be verbal responses or words. Words refer to conceptual categories; they are names of concepts. Thus the Kendlers' theory implies that insight is related to the use of concepts.

Perceptual set. Perceptual set is also related to concepts. Perceptual set means that previous experience determines how present events are perceived. For example, Murray (1933) asked 11-year-old girls to rate photographs of men and women after playing the game of "Murder" and after emotionally neutral experiences. After the game of "Murder" the girls rated most of the photographs as more cruel, malicious, and wicked; after the neutral experiences they rated them as more generous, kind, loving, and tender.

Solley (1966) asked young children to draw pictures of Santa Claus before and after Christmas. "As Christmas drew near, . . . their drawings of Santa became larger and larger . . . the bag with the toys and presents became more pronounced. . . . After Christmas . . . Santa was perceived as shrunken in size, plainer, and less significant" (pp. 288-289). Note that in Solley's study it appears that a future event is determining the pre-Christmas perceptions of Santa Claus. Actually, however, it is the child's anticipation of Christmas that is effective, and this anticipation depends on past experience.

Another kind of perceptual-set study also shows the effect of anticipation or expectancy on perception. In this kind of study the subject is shown a series of unambiguous figures, one at a time, and is asked to name each one. Then he is shown an ambiguous figure and is asked to name it. For example, the subject might be shown line drawings of various animals and then the picture in Figure 7.4. It has been found that subjects who are shown the animal figures first tend to see a mouse or rat in this picture. Subjects who are shown line drawings of human faces tend to see a bald-headed man wearing glasses. The unambiguous figures establish a set or expectancy to see more figures from the same conceptual category—animals or faces—and this expectancy influences the way the ambiguous figure is perceived.

It has also been found that the set becomes easier to establish with increasing age level. Very young children show little or no evidence of perceptual set. Even after seeing as many as 12 unambiguous figures, all from the same conceptual category, very young children often show no evidence of expecting to see another figure from the same category. Older children, in contrast, can be "set" by as few as six training pictures, and college students can be set by as few as one training picture. As in the case of insight, this developmental trend is believed to be related to the development of linguistic skill (see Reese, 1970c).

Figure 7.4
An ambiguous figure that is usually seen as a mouse or as a bald-headed man.

After Bugelski, B. R., & Alampay, D. A. The role of frequency in developing perceptual sets. *Canadian Journal of Psychology,* 1961, 15, Fig. 1, p. 206. Used by permission of the author and publisher.

Cognitive set. The phrase *cognitive set* is sometimes used to include perceptual set. This usage emphasizes the cognitive nature of perceptual set—the identification of the concept common to the training pictures and the development of an expectancy that more examples of the concept will be presented. However, cognitive set also refers to a more purely cognitive task in which previous experience with problem-solving has an influence on the way present problems are solved. The usual demonstration of cognitive set is to show that the previous mode of solution will be applied even when it is not the simplest solution.

Examples of cognitive set. For example, in a problem called the "Luchins jars problem" subjects are given jars with different capacities and are asked to pour water from jar to jar to obtain a required amount of water. One jar might contain 15 units and another 2 units. To obtain 11 units you would have to fill the larger jar and from it fill the smaller jar twice to leave 11 in the larger jar. In most of the research water is not actually poured from jar to jar, because of the mess. Instead, researchers usually use "thought" experiments in which subjects are instructed to pretend that they are pouring. Thus subjects are usually given the problems in word form and are asked for a verbal solution.

Examples of the jar problems are shown in Table 7.3. The first three can be solved in only one way, and in the same way for all three problems. The largest jar, B, must be filled, then poured once into Jar A and twice into Jar C to obtain the required amount, D. The equation is:

$$D = B - A - 2C$$

(Equation 1)

The next three problems are examples of test problems. The first two test problems can be solved either by Equation 1 or by a simpler equation:

$$D = A - C$$

(Equation 2)

The last is an example of test problems that can be solved only by Equation 2. After solving the first three problems, subjects who use Equation 1 to solve the test problems are exhibiting cognitive set. College students are susceptible to the influence of cognitive set, and it has also been demonstrated in children. Even when subjects are told "Don't be blind!" when the test problems are presented, they still exhibit cognitive set. The reason is presumably that this mode of performing is economical. It requires a minimum of mental effort to apply old solutions to new problems, in contrast to solving each new problem independently. It also can be an efficient mode of performing, because in many cases the old solutions will work.

Cognitive set and learning set.   Cognitive set is a kind of learning set (see Chapter 4). It is acquired in a series of training problems, all with the same solution. Furthermore, the solution has a conceptual basis. Cognitive set is considered here instead of in Chapter 4 only because the training problems discussed in Chapter 4 involve discriminative learning, while cognitive set does not.

It follows that the practical uses of cognitive set are similar to those of learning set, but that cognitive set should be more generally useful. For example, if you are teaching the use of

---

Table 7.3
Examples of Luchins Jar Problems

| Problem | Capacity | | | Amount Required |
	Jar A	Jar B	Jar C	(D)
1	14	163	25	99
2	18	43	10	5
3	9	42	6	21
4	23	49	3	20
5	14	36	8	6
6	28	76	3	25

equations and you would like a pupil to *discover* their useful-ness rather than being instructed about it, you should present problems like the Luchins jar training problems. The pupil should soon discover the applicable equation, and with suitable encouragement he will verbalize it. In subsequent problems he will discover that this equation works and is therefore useful. After he learns this, however, the equation should be made incorrect. The materials should be arranged so that first one equation works, then a different equation is required, then another is required. This process should continue until the pupil learns a very general cognitive set: equations are generally useful, but no one equation will always work.

Concluding Remarks

Our principal theme—that cognitive processes play a role in most forms of learning—is evident again in this chapter. The uses of concepts considered here are clearly related to cognition. The subject transforms the material by coding it into conceptual categories in an attempt to make the material easier to remember. He can recombine what he knows, creatively and insightfully, to meet demands of a task. And he can use his expectancies about the task as a basis for selecting ways of attacking it. Thus the influence of cognition —thinking, deciding, selecting—is seen in the more complex tasks considered in this last chapter, just as we saw its influence on learning tasks discussed in earlier chapters.

In addition many of the processes that we considered earlier are related to the processes considered in this chapter. Examples are easy to find. We have already noted the relationship between learning set (Chapter 4) and cognitive set. There is also a relationship between the acquisition of concepts like those considered here and performance in the free-recall task. Clustering in free recall (Chapter 5) cannot occur unless the subject possesses concepts like these. Similarly, the acquired equivalence of cues (Chapter 6) can be analyzed as the formation of artificial concepts, using techniques like the ones dealt with here. We can even see simple conditioning (Chapter 2) and discriminative learning (Chapter 3) as involving concept identification and utilization. Conditioning and discriminative learning have been attributed to an awareness of the contingency between the signaling stimulus and eliciting stimulus, or between the response and the contingent stimulus, and to an awareness of the implications of such contingencies. Such "awareness" seems to be a case of concept identification. Therefore, we can interpret successful performance as resulting from concept identification and subsequent utilization. In short, success in a presumably complex form of learning (concepts) often seems to be a necessary precondition for success in apparently simpler forms of learning.

Summary of Conceptual Processes

Concept attainment. Conceptual processes include the learning of concepts and the utilization of concepts. Concept attainment is called concept *identification* when the task requires the subject to learn a new response to a concept that he already knows. It is called concept *formation* when the task requires learning the meaning of a concept not previously known to the subject.

Concept identification should be easier than concept formation. Both require analyzing stimuli and finding the common attributes that define the relevant concept. Both seem to begin with trying out old concepts, and therefore concept formation should be harder because it does not begin until the old concepts have been tried and found inappropriate. The available evidence suggests that concept identification is easier than concept formation, but this interpretation can be challenged because of the nature of the concepts used in the relevant research.

There is some evidence that visual imagery interferes with concept identification and concept formation, apparently because the rich details in visual images focus attention on peculiarities of the items and obscure what they have in common.

Finally, both concept identification and concept formation are more difficult for younger children than for older children and adults. Among the possible causes of this developmental trend are: (1) The younger child is less attentive to stimulus attributes and examines them less systematically. (2) The younger child is slower to abandon attempted solutions that are incorrect. (3) The younger child may attain the concept but fail to produce it overtly and therefore fail to demonstrate that he has attained it.

Concepts as mediators.   In the mediation use of a concept a person uses a concept name to label an object or event and then responds to the label rather than to the object or event per se. Stereotyping is a typical example.

Concepts as codes.   In the coding use of a concept the concept name is applied to an object or event as an aid to memory. Memory may or may not be improved, depending upon whether the memory task requires that general or specific meanings be remembered. If general meanings are to be remembered, then conceptual coding aids memory, because concepts refer to generalized meanings. Adults use concept names as memory codes more than children do. Therefore, adults are inferior to children in tasks that require remembering specific meanings and are superior to children in tasks that require remembering general meanings.

Concepts as sets. Conceptual set includes several categories of effects. In *functional fixedness* there is an inability to extend the meaning of a concept to incorporate new functions or uses. Creativity implies an ability to overcome functional fixedness. Creativity increases with age, like other intellectual abilities. Conversely, functional fixedness decreases with increasing age.

In one kind of *insight* the subject must discover which of his already-acquired behavior sequences is appropriate in a given task. This kind of insight is analogous to concept identification. It occurs even in subhuman species and at young age levels. The other kind of insight requires that already-acquired behaviors be combined in novel ways to solve the problem presented. This kind does not occur in rats or young children, but it does occur and improve with increasing age in humans. It is thought to be related to language development in that it is related to the use of words as representational responses.

Perceptual set means that previous experience determines how present events are perceived. Expecting to see a particular kind of event increases the likelihood that the event will in fact be perceived, but the perception may not be objectively accurate. Perceptual sets become easier to establish with increasing age level. This developmental trend is believed to be related to language development.

In *cognitive set* problem-solving is influenced by previous experience with similar problems. Cognitive set is like learning set in this respect, and, like learning set, it is an economical and efficient process if the new problem has the same solution as the training problems. There are very general cognitive sets that do not refer to specific solutions but to ways of attacking problems. Thus the use of a specific equation in attempting to solve a problem is a cognitive set, but so is the general strategy of using equations.

Conclusion. The formation, identification, and utilization of concepts seem to be pervasive through most of the apparently simpler forms of learning which we have considered in earlier chapters.

Suggested Readings

Concept Attainment

Flavell, J. H. Concept development. In P. H. Mussen (Ed.), *Carmichael's manual of child psychology.* (3rd ed.) Vol. I. New York: Wiley, 1970.

Concept Utilization

Kendler, T. S., & Kendler, H. H. Experimental analysis of inferential behavior in children. In L. P. Lipsitt & C. C.

Spiker (Eds.), *Advances in child development and behavior*. Vol. 3. New York: Academic Press, 1967.

Reese, H. W. Set. In H. W. Reese & L. P. Lipsitt (Eds.), *Experimental child psychology*. New York: Academic Press, 1970.

Uznadze, D. N. *The psychology of set*. New York: Consultants Bureau, 1966.

References

References

Baer, D. M., & Sherman, J. A. Behavior modification: Clinical and educational applications. In H. W. Reese & L. P. Lipsitt (Eds.), *Experimental child psychology*. New York: Academic Press, 1970. Pp. 643-672.

Bugelski, B. R., & Alampay, D. A. The role of frequency in developing perceptual sets. *Canadian Journal of Psychology*, 1961, 15, 205-211.

Carmichael, L., Hogan, H. P., & Walter, A. A. An experimental study of the effect of language on the reproduction of visually perceived form. *Journal of Experimental Psychology*, 1932, 15, 73-86.

Cautela, J. R. Covert conditioning. In A. Jacobs & L. B. Sachs (Eds.), *The psychology of private events: Perspectives on covert response systems*. New York: Academic Press, 1971. Pp. 109-130.

Corsini, D. A. Developmental changes in the effect of non-verbal cues on retention. *Developmental Psychology*, 1969, 1, 425-435.

Flavell, J. H. Developmental studies of mediated memory. In H. W. Reese & L. P. Lipsitt (Eds.), *Advances in child development and behavior*. Vol. 5. New York; Academic Press, 1970. Pp. 181-211.

Forbes, E. J., & Reese, H. W. Pictorial elaboration and recall of multilist paired associates. *Journal of Experimental Psychology*, 1974, 102, 836-840.

Gellermann, L. W. Chance orders of alternating stimuli in visual discrimination experiments. *Journal of Genetic Psychology*, 1933, 42, 206-208

Harlow, H. F. Analysis of discrimination learning by monkeys. *Journal of Experimental Psychology*, 1950, 40, 26-39.

Harlow, H. F. Learning set and error factor theory. In S. Koch (Ed.), *Psychology: A study of a science*. Vol. 2. New York: McGraw-Hill, 1959. Pp. 492-537.

Hollenberg, C. K. Functions of visual imagery in the learning and concept formation of children. *Child Development*, 1970, 41, 1003-1015.

Hovland, C. I. Human learning and retention. In S. S. Stevens (Ed.), *Handbook of experimental psychology*. New York: Wiley, 1951. Pp. 613-689.

Jacobs, A., & Wolpin, M. A second look at systematic desensitization. In A. Jacobs & L. B. Sachs (Eds.), *The psychology of private events: Perspectives on covert response systems*. New York: Academic Press, 1971. Pp. 77-108.

Kendler, T. S. An ontogeny of mediational deficiency. *Child Development*, 1972, 43, 1-17.

Kendler, T. S., & Kendler, H. H. Experimental analysis of inferential behavior in children. In L. P. Lipsitt & C. C. Spiker (Eds.), *Advances in child development and behavior*. Vol. 3. New York: Academic Press, 1967. Pp. 157-190.

Koffka, K. Perception: An introduction to the *Gestalt-Theorie*. *Psychological Bulletin*, 1922, 19, 531-585.

Koppenaal, R. J., Krull, A., & Katz, H. Age, interference, and forgetting. *Journal of Experimental Child Psychology*, 1964, 1, 360-375.

Lashley, K. S. The mechanism of vision. XV. Preliminary studies of the rat's capacity for detailed vision. *Journal of General Psychology,* 1938, 18, 123-193.

Lee, L. C. Concept utilization in preschool children. *Child Development,* 1965, 36, 221-227.

Levin, J. R. Inducing comprehension in poor readers: A test of a recent model. *Journal of Educational Psychology,* 1973, 65, 19-24.

Levinson, B., & Reese, H. W. Patterns of discrimination learning set in preschool children, fifth-graders, college freshmen, and the aged. *Monographs of the Society for Research in Child Development,* 1967, 32 (7, Whole No. 115).

Lipsitt, L. P., Kaye, H., & Bosack, T. N. Enhancement of neonatal sucking through reinforcement. *Journal of Experimental Child Psychology,* 1966, 4, 163-168.

Longstreth, L. E. *Psychological development of the child.* New York: Ronald Press, 1968.

Maier, N. R. F. Reasoning in humans. II. The solution of a problem and its appearance in consciousness. *Journal of Comparative Psychology,* 1931, 12, 181-194.

Murray, H. A. The effect of fear upon estimates of the maliciousness of other personalities. *Journal of Social Psychology,* 1933, 4, 310-329.

Nikkel, N., & Palermo, D. S. Effects of mediated associations in paired-associate learning of children. *Journal of Experimental Child Psychology,* 1965, 2, 92-102.

Norcross, K. J., & Spiker, C. C. The effects of mediated associations on transfer in paired-associate learning. *Journal of Experimental Psychology,* 1958, 55, 129-134.

Paivio, A. *Imagery and verbal processes.* New York: Holt, Rinehart and Winston, 1971.

Reese, H. W. The distance effect in transposition in the intermediate size problem. *Journal of Comparative and Physiological Psychology,* 1962, 55, 528-531. (a)

Reese, H. W. Verbal mediation as a function of age level. *Psychological Bulletin,* 1962, 59, 502-509. (b)

Reese, H. W. Discrimination learning set in children. In L. P. Lipsitt & C. C Spiker (Eds.), *Advances in child development and behavior.* Vol. 1. New York: Academic Press, 1963.

Pp. 115-145.

Reese, H. W. Discrimination learning set in rhesus monkeys. *Psychological Bulletin,* 1964, 61, 321-340.

Reese, H. W. Imagery in paired-associate learning in children. *Journal of Experimental Child Psychology,* 1965, 2, 290-296.

Reese H. W. *The perception of stimulus relations: Discrimination learning and transposition.* New York: Academic Press, 1968.

Reese, H. W. Imagery in children's paired-associate learning. *Journal of Experimental Child Psychology,* 1970, 9, 174-178. (a)

Reese, H. W. Imagery and contextual meaning. In H. W. Reese (Chm.). Imagery in children's learning: A symposium. *Psychological Bulletin,* 1970, 73, 404-414. (b)

Reese, H. W. Set. In H. W. Reese & L. P. Lipsitt (Eds.), *Experimental child psychology.* New York: Academic Press, 1970. Pp. 263-278. (c)

Reese, H. W. Acquired distinctiveness and equivalence of cues in young children. *Journal of Experimental Child Psychology,* 1972, 13, 171-182.

Reese, H. W. Verbal effects in children's visual recognition-memory. *Child Development,* 1975, 46, 400-407.

Reese, H. W., & Parkington, J. J. Intralist interference and imagery in deaf and hearing children. *Journal of Experimental Child Psychology,* 1973, 16, 165-183.

Rohwer, W. D., Jr. Elaboration and learning in childhood and adolescence. In H. W. Reese (Ed.), *Advances in child development and behavior.* Vol. 8. New York: Academic Press, 1973. Pp. 1-57.

Rossi, E. L. Development of classificatory behavior. *Child Development,* 1964, 35, 137-142.

Sameroff, A. J. Can conditioned responses be established in the newborn infant: 1971? *Developmental Psychology,* 1971, 4, 1-12.

Sameroff, A. J. Learning and adaptation in infancy: A comparison of models. In H. W. Reese (Ed.), *Advances in child development and behavior.* Vol. 7. New York: Academic Press, 1972. Pp. 169-214.

Seltzer, R. J. Effects of reinforcement and deprivation on the development of non-nutritive sucking in monkeys and humans. Unpublished doctoral dissertation, Brown University, 1968.

Shepp, B. E. Some cue properties of anticipated rewards in discrimination learning of retardates. *Journal of Comparative and Physiological Psychology,* 1962, 55, 856-859.

Siqueland, E. R. Instrumental conditioning in infants. In H. W. Reese & L. P. Lipsitt (Eds.), *Experimental child psychology.* New York: Academic Press, 1970. Pp. 102-123.

Solley, C. M. Affective processes in perceptual development. In A. H. Kidd & J. L. Rivoire (Eds.), *Perceptual development in children.* New York: International Universities Press, 1966. Pp. 275-304.

Spence, K. W. Cognitive factors in the extinction of the conditioned eyelid response in humans. *Science,* 1963, 140, 1224-1225.

Spiker, C. C. Performance on a difficult discrimination following pretraining with distinctive stimuli. *Child Development,* 1959, 30, 513-521.

Spiker, C. C. Associative transfer in verbal paired-associate learning. *Child Development,* 1960, 31, 73-87.

Tighe, L. W., Schechter, J., & Tighe, T. Memory for instances and categories in children and adults. Paper presented at the meeting of the Psychonomic Society, St. Louis, November 1973.

Underwood, B. J. *Experimental psychology: An introduction.* Englewood Cliffs, N. J.: Prentice-Hall, 1949. Originally published by Appleton-Century-Crofts.

Weisberg, P., & Simmons, M. W. A modified WGTA for infants in their second year of life. *Journal of Psychology,* 1966, 63, 99-104.

Witryol, S. L. Incentives and learning in children. In H. W. Reese (Ed.), *Advances in child development and behavior.* Vol. 6. New York: Academic Press, 1971. Pp. 1-61.

Index